Nora Newton

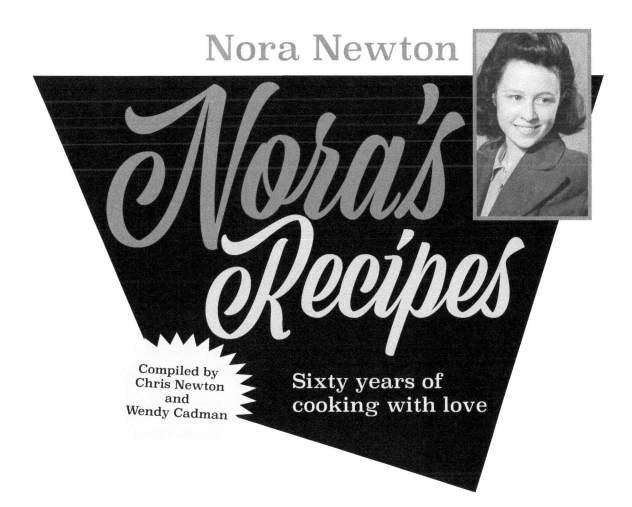

Nora's Recipes

Compiled by
Chris Newton
and
Wendy Cadman

Sixty years of
cooking with love

Nora Newton

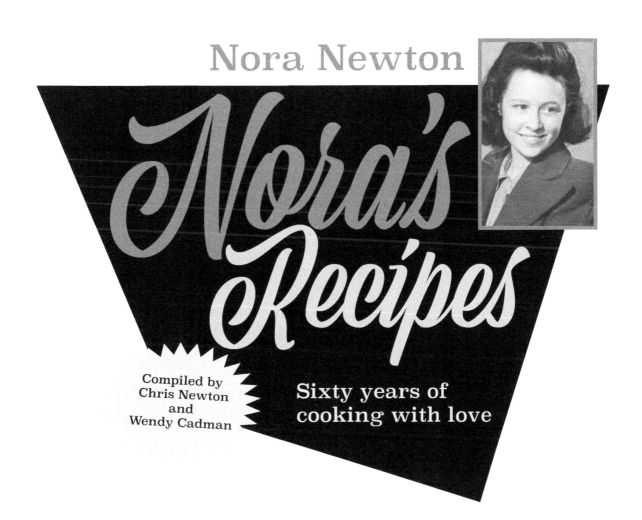

Nora's Recipes

Compiled by
Chris Newton
and
Wendy Cadman

Sixty years of
cooking with love

Mereo Books

1A The Wool Market Dyer Street Cirencester Gloucestershire GL7 2PR
An imprint of Memoirs Publishing www.mereobooks.com

First published in Great Britain in 2017
by Mereo Books, an imprint of Memoirs Publishing

ISBN: 978-1-86151-778-4

Copyright ©2017

The address for Memoirs Publishing Group Limited can be found at www.memoirspublishing.com

The Memoirs Publishing Group Ltd Reg. No. 7834348

The Memoirs Publishing Group supports both The Forest Stewardship Council® (FSC®) and the
PEFC® leading international forest-certification organisations. Our books carrying both the FSC
label and the PEFC® and are printed on FSC®-certified paper. FSC® is the only
forest-certification scheme supported by the leading environmental organisations including
Greenpeace. Our paper procurement policy can be found at
www.memoirspublishing.com/environment

Typeset in 9/14pt Bembo
by Wiltshire Associates Publisher Services Ltd. Printed and bound in Great Britain by
Printondemand-Worldwide, Peterborough PE2 6XD

Foreword

I grew up in the 1950s and 60s, at a time when wartime rationing was still fresh in everyone's minds and food cost far more than it does today. Waste was a sin, and obesity unusual. Both Mum and Gran exhorted us to eat bread and butter with every meal 'to make it go further'.

The food served on the dining tables of the nation was still overwhelmingly English, and I can remember the excitement and the tension when one evening towards the end of the 1950s, Mum served something we had never heard of called 'Spaghetti Bolognese'. It was a startlingly different dish from the Heinz tinned spaghetti we were used to, but to her great relief Dad, Martin, Heather and I (Simon had not yet arrived) all agreed that it was far superior, and it became a regular fixture from then on. The only Asian food I can remember from that time was Vesta Chow Mein, sold as a DIY kit of paper packets containing dried ingredients. We thought it was delicious, though to modern tastes it would be about as haute cuisine as a Pot Noodle. Of course, none of the supermarkets now sell it, but guess what – I've just checked, and you can buy it from Amazon.

More traditional dishes I remember from those days included what we called 'Saturday Soup', an irresistible consommé made as a by-product of boiling a joint of beef. Mum doesn't appear to have left the recipe, sadly, but I suppose it was little more than beef stock and seasoning. Another massive hit was the spectacular pork pie she used to make at Christmas, fabulously lean and crumbly. If you have only eaten shop-bought pork pies, never mind how rustically elitist the label, I promise that one taste of Mum's would be epiphanic. Unfortunately it was so good that all the guests rushed back for more, and the pie she had expected to feed the family with for two or three days was reduced to crumbs within hours. Again, no recipe to be found. The secret has gone with her, like Fermat's proof of his Last Theorem.

I have been reincarnating Mum's stew and hotpot dishes (or trying to) ever since I left home nearly fifty years ago, although I have tried and failed to reproduce the delicious light risotto (strictly a savoury rice dish, I suppose, not a proper Italian-style risotto) which she used to knock up in minutes. This recipe is not lost – it's in this book, and I will be trying it soon.

Mum and I had several adventures with fish as a result of my angling exploits, and I can remember frying plaice, pollack and mackerel with her in Cornwall within minutes, and yards, of their capture, and developing a successful recipe for pike pie (the pike being a fish which needs a little help to make it as palatable as say cod or trout).

Mum was greatly influenced in her cooking adventures by her big sister, Auntie Marjorie, who adored French cooking and did a great deal of it. Marjorie could be a little lofty towards her younger sister sometimes, but I think she taught her quite a lot and certainly she persuaded her to be more adventurous. Mum's interest in French cooking was encouraged by three French family holidays in 1977 (with Marjorie & Co), 1983 and 1994, the only occasions when she ever travelled abroad.

Mum owned many cookery books, notably the works of Elizabeth David, Jane Grigson, Marguerite Patten and naturally Mrs Beeton, but she was drawn to newer writers too and books by Jamie Oliver, Gary Rhodes and Nigel Slater stood among the dog-eared older volumes. I well remember her *schadenfreude* when the snobbish, overbearing Fanny Cradock was sacked by the BBC after she was unforgivably rude to an amateur cook from Devon about a menu she offered on TV.

Mum was an inveterate collector of clippings on subjects which interested her, such as history, literature and the arts, and cooking was no exception; whenever you opened one of her cookbooks a recipe from a newspaper or magazine would be sure to fall out. The two volumes of hand-written recipes which are reproduced in this book were full of them. I'm sure she would be quite astonished to see her own recipes in print, as her opinion of her own skills was always far too modest.

The recipes here have not been reworded (Mum's English was perfect anyway of course) as I was keen to retain her own style and the modesty and lack of didacticism of her writing. I have left out a number which she credited to the pros, but all the rest are included. In a few cases she has given very similar recipes twice, so I have omitted one of them. However it's clear that in other cases the recipes were designed to be different, such as her two recipes for chocolate cake. I don't remember Mum baking a chocolate cake which wasn't fabulous, so these are presumably good in different ways.

Mum cooked for the family with unlimited love and dedication, as well as great skill and imagination, virtually every day from her marriage to Dad in 1948 until the time, more than sixty years later, when she could no longer cope with living at home. We owe her an enormous debt.

Chris
February 2017

Nora's Recipes
by Nora Newton

1929-2015

Dedicated to the memory of Mum and Dad.
Would that all marriages were as happy, long
and loving as theirs.

With thanks to my partner Wendy, for
suggesting this project and then
doing the heroic job of typing up the recipes.

Contents

SAUCES, VEGETABLES & MISCELLANEOUS

3 - CAKES AND PUDDINGS

OTHER SWEET DISHES AND ACCOMPANIMENTS

Soups & Starters

Cream of Potato Soup

- 1lb peeled potatoes
- 1 pint chicken stock
- 2 large onions
- Bay leaf
- Seasoning
- Pinch celery salt

- 2ozs butter
- 1oz flour
- 1 pint milk
- Half pint single cream
- Pinch cayenne pepper
- A little chopped parsley

Serve Very Hot

Cut the potatoes into small pieces and put into the stock with the chopped onion, bay leaf and seasoning. Cook gently until tender. Put through a sieve. Heat the butter in a saucepan, stir in the flour, cook for a few minutes then gradually stir in the milk. Bring to the boil and simmer gently until a smooth thickened sauce. Add the potato puree, heat, then stir in the cream, seasonings, cayenne and celery salt.

Golden Soup

- 1lb carrots
- 1 medium onion
- 1 potato (about 6ozs)
- 2ozs butter
- 2 pints chicken stock*
- Half teaspoon thyme or a bouquet garni
- Quarter pint single cream
- Small teaspoon sugar

Peel and thinly slice the carrots and onion. Melt the butter in a large saucepan, add the vegetables and fry gently, with the pan covered, for about 10 minutes, until they are soft but not brown. Pour in the stock, then add the potato, peeled and diced. Add the thyme or bouquet garni and seasonings and sugar. Stir well and bring to simmering point. Cook gently for about 1 hour. Sieve, return to the pan and re-heat, then stir in the cream. Check the seasonings and serve very hot but do not allow to boil after the cream has been added.

I think that rather than sieve all the soup, I would sieve about one third and then add to the remainder. The texture is better and the flavour very good. Some finely-sliced celery green is a good addition to the vegetables.

Remember to remove the bouquet garni, bay leaves, etc before liquidising!

*I use 1½ chicken cubes for this amount of stock.

Mushroom Soup 1

Peel and finely slice a medium onion. Peel and dice a small potato. Wash and cut up half pound of small mushrooms. Melt about 2ozs butter in a pan, add the onion and potato and fry gently until soft and lightly coloured. Add the mushrooms and cook gently for a short time, shaking the pan from time to time. Pour in about one and a half pints of stock (made from a chicken cube), stir gently and bring to simmering point. Season with salt and pepper, add a bouquet garni, and cook gently (covered) for about three quarters to one hour. Take about a quarter to a half pint milk, take a little of this and set aside. Add the remainder to the pan. Stir a good tablespoon flour into the reserved milk, mix to a smooth texture and stir into the pan. Continue to simmer gently until cooked. Serve into bowls, pouring a little single cream into each one.

Mushroom Soup 2

- ✺ Half lb mushrooms
- ✺ 1 onion
- ✺ 1 pint of stock
- ✺ 1oz of butter
- ✺ 1oz of flour
- ✺ Three quarters pint of milk
- ✺ Salt & pepper
- ✺ Single cream

Wipe and slice the mushrooms and chop the onion. Melt the butter in a fairly large saucepan and sauté the mushrooms and onion for about 2-3 minutes until soft. Pour in the stock. Blend the flour with a little of the milk and add gradually to the soup with the rest of the milk. Season to taste. Bring to the boil stirring all the while and then simmer gently for three quarters – 1 hour.

*Add the cream before serving, but do not let the soup boil.

*I generally make this soup fairly early in the day, or the day before it is served. Before the final re-heating I take about half the soup from the pan and liquidise it in my blender, then return it to the pan before re-heating. I think it gives it a better consistency and flavour, the addition of the flour mixture is scarcely necessary.

Onion Soup

- ✳ 2 fairly large onions (about ¾lb)
- ✳ 1½ pints beef stock
- ✳ Butter (1-2ozs)
- ✳ Dry sherry

Peel the onions and slice them very finely. Fry gently in butter until golden. Pour in the stock (I use if possible vegetable water to dilute 1 beef cube, left-over gravy can be useful too). Bring to the boil, simmer very gently with pot covered for about three quarters to one hour*. Check seasonings and add a wineglass of dry sherry. If liked serve sprinkled with finely grated cheese. Warm garlic bread is good to accompany.

*I liquidise the soup at this stage but only about half of it, to liquidise all tends to give a rather boring consistency.

Main Courses

2

A Dish of Fillet Steaks

- ✳ 1 fillet steak per person
- ✳ 1-2 onions
- ✳ 4-8ozs mushrooms
- ✳ Stock
- ✳ Butter
- ✳ Single cream

Melt an ounce or two of butter in a frying pan and fry the steaks for a minute or two on both sides. Remove from the pan and fry the sliced onions, adding a little more butter if necessary. Remove the onions and add the sliced mushrooms. Put the onions and mushrooms into a shallow oven-proof dish and place the steaks on top, seasoning all with salt and black pepper and adding one or two bay leaves. Add a little flour to the juices in the pan, stir until smooth and add gradually sufficient stock to make a good gravy. When smooth and boiling remove from the heat and stir in about 3 or 4 tablespoons of single cream. Pour over the steaks, place in the centre of the oven (Gas No. 4) and cook for about 1 hour.

A Simple Dish of Chicken Breasts

I took 4 chicken breasts and laid them skin side down in a roasting tin containing an ounce or two of hot melted butter (or good dripping or oil). I seasoned the underside with salt and pepper, a sprinkling of herbs and chopped parsley. I turned them over and sprinkled the skin side with seasonings and herbs. I had prepared 3 or 4 smallish potatoes and had boiled them for a few minutes and drained them. I cut these into thick slices, dipped them in the melted butter and arranged them around the chicken. I put the dish in the oven, gas mark 6, for about an hour, turning the meat over halfway through. I made a gravy with the juices in the pan and served the breasts with a mushroom sauce (a few mushrooms thinly sliced and cooked in water for a few minutes, then stirred into a white sauce).

Variation: I cooked the breasts in hot butter for a few minutes and dipped the potato slices in the butter*. I then cooked 4ozs sliced mushrooms in the butter and made a sauce in the pan, using chicken stock and milk.

Baked Lamb Chops
(Marjorie's recipe)

* 6 large lamb chops
* 3 onions
* 12 medium potatoes
* A little stock (about ¼ pint)
* Parsley
* Butter
* Seasonings
* Garlic

Brown the chops in a little butter. Chop the onions finely and cook in butter until golden. Slice the raw potatoes into fine rounds and mix with the onions, a little chopped parsley, salt and pepper. Rub a buttered ovenproof dish with garlic and put in a layer of the potatoes, then the chops, then cover with the rest of the potatoes. Moisten with about 1 cup of stock (or water) and cook in a moderate oven for about 1½ hours.

Baked Stuffed Onions

* 4 large onions
* ½ lb good minced beef (raw)
* ½ oz dripping
* 2 dessertspoons tomato ketchup

Place the unpeeled onions in a saucepan of boiling water, bring back to the boil and simmer gently for about 10 minutes. Drain, then peel the outer skins off the onions and cut off their tops. With a teaspoon scoop out the inner part, leaving a thick outer shell. Chop this inner part and mix with the minced beef. Fry gently until browned, then stir in the ketchup, seasonings and a pinch of mixed herbs. Fill each onion with the mixture. Wrap each in cooking foil and place in a baking tin. Bake at mark 4 for about 1¼ hours.

Beef Casserole

* ¾ lb rump steak
* 2 lambs' kidneys
* 3-4 ozs unsmoked streaky bacon
* A medium onion and a few shallots
* 2-3 ozs mushrooms

Melt an ounce of two of butter, brown the sliced onion and the bacon (cut into small pieces). Remove from the pan and brown the mushrooms, also cut into pieces until very small. Remove these also (the onion, bacon and mushrooms can all be browned together) and put the meat (well trimmed and cut into pieces) into the pan. Brown the meat, sprinkle in 2 tablespoons of flour and brown this. Add half pint of good stock, stir well until smooth and simmering, stir in the onions, bacon and mushrooms and add a quarter pint of red wine. Add the shallots, seasonings and a bouquet garni. Simmer for about 3 hours at Gas no. 2. Good idea to prepare the day before wanted, cook for about 2 hours and 1 hour before serving.

Beef & Ham Roll
(Gran's recipe)

- ✸ ½ lb ham or lean bacon
- ✸ ½ lb lean steak
- ✸ 2 slices bread
- ✸ 2 small eggs
- ✸ Seasonings

Trim the ham and steak and mince together. Mix together with breadcrumbs, add salt and pepper and a pinch of mixed herbs. Break the egg into the mixture and stir all well together. Pack into an earthenware jar, cover and steam for about two hours in a saucepan of boiling water. Turn out when cool and serve sliced when thoroughly cold.

Beef in Dairy Cream

- 1½ lbs stewing steak
- 1oz plain flour
- 1oz dripping
- ½ lb carrots
- 8 spring onions
- 2-3 turnips
- Quarter pint single cream
- Cold water
- Salt & pepper

Cut the meat into small pieces and coat with the flour. Fry in the dripping till browned. Add the sliced onions, cook a little longer. Stir in enough water just to cover the meat, cover and simmer for 1 hour. Add the diced vegetables, simmer for another 30 mins. Stir in the cream and seasonings before serving.

Boeuf Bourguignon

- 1-1½ lbs lean topside or braising steak
- 8ozs button onions
- 1 bay leaf
- Sprig fresh thyme or parsley
- ½ pint Burgundy wine
- 3 tablespoons oil
- 4 rashers streaky bacon, cut into strips
- 1 clove of garlic, crushed
- 6ozs button mushrooms
- 1-2 tablespoons cornflour
- 1 beef stock cube
- ¼ pint boiling water
- Bouquet garni, seasonings

Trim the steak and cut into small pieces. Place the onions, herbs & wine in a bowl, cover and marinate for up to 12 hours. Heat the oil in a flameproof casserole, sauté the bacon, onion & garlic and brown the meat well. Stir in the cornflour and cook for 1-2 minutes, Pour in the strained marinade and stock. Bring to the boil, stirring. Add the bouquet garni and mushrooms, cover and cook at gas no. 3 for 2 hours. Remove the bouquet garni, adjust seasoning and sprinkle with chopped parsley.

Boiled Bacon

* Piece of collar bacon about 2-2½ lbs
* small bay leaf
* 6 peppercorns

Cover the bacon with plenty of cold water and leave to soak overnight. Drain off the liquid and cover with fresh cold water, adding the bay leaf and peppercorns. Bring to the boil with the pan uncovered, and when boiling skin off any foam. Put the lid on the pan and simmer gently (too-fast cooking toughens the meat) for the required time, allowing 20 minutes to the pound and 20 minutes extra. When cooked, leave to go cold in the liquid, then drain and remove the rind. Serve cold, sliced thinly with a green salad or vegetables.

Boiled Ham

Scrape the entire surface of the ham with the edge of a knife-blade in order to remove any dust or impurities. Place the ham in a large saucepan and cover with plain cold water. Bring to the boil, cover the pan, and simmer gently until the meat is tender (a piece costing 10-12s. Will need about 2 hours).* Cool in the liquid. Lift the meat from the pan, drain well and strip off the outer rind. Leave to cool, then coat the fat with crisp golden breadcrumbs. The ham should be thinly sliced when quite cold, and served with a salad or vegetables.

*20 minutes per 1lb of weight plus 20 minutes extra.

Boiled Leg of Lamb
(Marjorie's recipe)

- ✳ Leg of lamb 2-3lbs
- ✳ 4 carrots (not too big)
- ✳ 2 onions
- ✳ 2 small turnips
- ✳ 1 leek
- ✳ Seasonings and herbs
- ✳ (No stock cube is needed)

Place the lamb in a flameproof casserole and add about 2 pints of water. Add the onions, peeled but left whole, 2 whole cloves of garlic, salt and pepper and a faggot of herbs (bay leaf, parsley, thyme, rosemary, etc or as you please). Simmer gently for about half an hour or so, then add the peeled and sliced carrots and turnips and the cleaned and sliced leek. Continue simmering for about another 1½ – 2 hours. Remove the meat and put in a warm place. Strain off about half a pint or so of the liquid and make a sauce with butter, flour and the liquid, adding about 4 tablespoons of single cream when it is smooth and simmering. Any surplus liquid from the meat makes a delicious soup.

Boulangère Potatoes

* 2 onions
* 3lbs old potatoes
* 3ozs butter
* Salt and ground black pepper
* 1 pint chicken stock

Peel the onions and potatoes and slice both thinly. Melt 1oz butter in a pan, add the onions. Cook for a few minutes until soft. Butter a 3 pint pie dish with the remaining butter, arrange the potatoes and onions in layers. Season well with salt and pepper. Arrange the top layer of potatoes in overlapping slices, pour the stock over. Bake at Gas no 5 for about one and a half hours until tender.

Braised Steak

Cut 1lb rump steak into about 6 pieces and slice up 2 lambs' kidneys. Fry a thinly-sliced medium onion in 2ozs butter, remove and place in a casserole. Season the meat and cook on both sides in the butter until brown, then place on the onions. Peel and slice ¼ lb mushrooms, fry these in the butter and add the casserole. Stir a small spoonful of flour into the remaining butter, then stir in gradually ¾ pint of stock, made with a beef or chicken cube. When this boils, pour it over the contents of the casserole, scraping the bottom of the pan well to remove all the sediment. Season with salt and pepper and a pinch of mixed herbs and add 2 tablespoons of red wine. Cook at Mark 2 for 1½–2 hours.

Chicken Casserole (1)

Take 3 or 4 chicken breast fillets, skin them and cut each into fairly large pieces. Fry the skins (I used my round red French casserole), turning them as they crisp and brown, then discard. Fry the breast pieces in the fat, having rolled them in seasoned and herbed flour, until they are slightly browned. Add a little butter to the pan, as needed. Remove the meat, add a large onion (or 2 smaller ones), previously sliced, and half a dozen mushrooms washed and sliced. When these are softened and coloured add the chicken to the casserole, together with three quarters pint of stock. Also add one or two carrots, some washed and sliced celery green, a few shallots or other vegetables to your taste. Bring to simmering point and cook very gently for 1½ to 2 hours. Add herbs and seasonings to taste. If the liquid seems rather thin, mix together some butter and flour (about half ounce of each, until creamed smooth, break off small pieces and add to the casserole about 10-15 minutes before serving.

Chicken Casserole (2)

* 1 small chicken (or 4 chicken joints)
* 2ozs butter
* Quarter pound mushrooms
* 1 large or several tiny onions
* 1 carrot
* Half pint stock or water (or three quarter pint of stock and quarter pint milk
* Half pint milk
* 1 chicken stock cube

Season the chicken with salt and pepper. Melt the butter and fry the chicken or joints all over until golden. Place in a casserole. Slice the onions if large (use whole if tiny) and slice and peel the mushrooms. Fry these in the hot butter until soft and add to the casserole. Stir 1oz flour into the remaining butter (adding a little more if necessary), then stir into it gradually the liquid, consisting of half pint of hot water or stock into which one chicken cube has been dissolved and half pint of milk. When the sauce is smooth and boiling add salt, pepper, a good pinch of mixed herbs, a bay leaf and a diced carrot. Pour this over the chicken, cover the casserole and cook for 2-3 hours at Mark 4.

Chicken Pie (1)

- ✹ 6-8ozs cold cooked chicken
- ✹ 4-6ozs mushrooms
- ✹ 8ozs shortcrust pastry
- ✹ Seasonings etc
- ✹ Milk

Wash and slice the mushrooms and cook in a little butter for a few minutes. Add some flour to the pan, cook for a moment or two, then gradually stir in sufficient milk to make a thick sauce. Season well and simmer gently for 2 or 3 minutes. Stir in the chicken, which should be cut into fairly small pieces, well trimmed and with no undesirable bits. You can also stir in a few cold cooked garden peas, runner beans, carrots etc if you have them. Leave the mixture to cool. Line an 8" pie plate with half the pastry, put in the chicken filling, put on the remainder of the pastry rolled to form a lid. Decorate as you like and chill if possible. Brush with beaten egg and bake at Gas No 6, upper part of the oven, until golden brown.

Chicken Pie (2)

I took 2 quarter pieces (breast) of chicken and put into a large pan. I added a piece of leek, a stick of celery, a carrot and an onion, all peeled and sliced. I covered these with water and added seasonings and a bouquet garni (no stock cube). I bought these to simmering point and simmered on a low heat for around an hour. When cooled (I left it overnight) I took all skin and bone from the chicken and cut all the flesh into pieces. I added some of the vegetables to the meat and made about half pint of white sauce, using milk and a little stock from the pan. I stirred this into the chicken mix and left to cool.

I made 10ozs shortcrust pastry and used my largest enamel plate, lining it with half the pastry. I added the filling, covered it with a pastry lid and left in the fridge overnight. Brush with beaten egg, bake at Gas 6 for about 45 minutes. To accompany, I made half a pint of white sauce using a quarter pint of milk and a quarter pint of the stock.

Chicken Pie (3)

- ✳ Half a chicken
- ✳ 1 onion
- ✳ 1-2 carrots
- ✳ 2ozs mushrooms
- ✳ 6ozs short-crust pastry
- ✳ Milk
- ✳ seasonings.

Cook the chicken in butter or margarine until tender. Peel and slice the onion and the carrots and cook in salted water for 10-15 minutes. Add the sliced mushrooms and cook for a further 10-15 minutes, when the vegetables should be tender. Slice the chicken, removing all skin and bones. Make a little well-seasoned white sauce (rather less than half a pint), using the fat from the chicken pan as a basis. Add the vegetables and the chicken slices, and mix well. Line a pie-plate with half the pastry, pour in the filling and cover with the remaining pastry. Bake at Mark 5 (3rd runner down) for 20-30 minutes. Small quantities of various other cooked vegetables may be added to the white sauce, such as peas, beans, or chopped leeks.

Chicken Breasts

Take one chicken breast for each person. Remove the skin, place this in a baking tin and put into the oven at Gas No 5. This will draw the fat for cooking the breasts. Make some fine white breadcrumbs, season well with salt and pepper and add a generous sprinkling of dried herbs and/or chopped parsley.

Coat each breast with flour, then dip in beaten egg. Then coat each with the seasoned breadcrumbs.

Take the baking tin from the oven and add a good piece of butter to the fat from the skins. When melted, place each breast in the tin, turning each well to coat with the melted fat. Then cover with a greased paper and bake at Gas No 5 for about an hour, removing the paper for the last 20 minutes of the cooking time. Make an accompanying gravy or sauce, using the fat in the tin.

Chicken Paprika

- 1 small onion
- 2 medium chicken joints
- 1 tbsp cooking oil
- Half a 4oz tin red peppers (or use fresh one)
- 1 ½ oz flour
- 1 level tbsp paprika
- 1 rounded dessertsp tomato puree
- Half chicken cube
- Quarter pint boiling water
- Salt and pepper

Skin and roughly chop the onion. Wipe the chicken joints, fry the onion and chicken in oil for 10 minutes. Drain and slice the red peppers. Add the flour to the chicken with the peppers, paprika and tomato puree. Stir well. Dissolve the stock cube in the boiling water. Add to the pan. Season. Cover the pan tightly, and simmer for about 1 and half hours. Serve with mashed potatoes or rice.

Chicken Parcels
(for 4 people)

✳ 4 portions of chicken	✳ 1 gill dry cider or white stock
✳ 2 minced onions	✳ Chopped parsley
✳ 6ozs chopped mushrooms	✳ Thyme
✳ 1 gill double cream	✳ Salt and pepper

Season the portions of chicken with salt and pepper. Put each portion on a piece of kitchen foil and divide the remaining ingredients equally. Add to the parcels until covering the chicken portions. Wrap up very firmly. Put into a baking tin and bake at Mark 6 for 1 hour. Serve hot, or cold with salad.

Chicken Risotto
(very good with pork fillet instead of chicken)

* 1 medium onion
* 1 bunch spring onions
* 4ozs mushrooms
* Garlic cloves
* 2-4 chicken breasts
* Half green pepper
* Half red or yellow pepper
* 8ozs long grain rice
* Three quarters of a pint chicken stock

Melt one or two tablespoons good olive oil and an ounce of butter in a large frying pan. Peel and slice the onion, peel and chop 2-3 garlic cloves and fry these lightly. Meanwhile, trim and wash the spring onions and cut into half inch lengths. De-seed and wash the pepper halves and cut into small pieces. Remove the fried onion and garlic to a hot dish, add the spring onions and peppers to the pan, fry gently for a minute or so, then add to the dish. Add a little more butter to the pan if needed. Wash the mushrooms, cut into pieces if large and fry for a few minutes, then add to the dish. Cut the chicken breasts into pieces and fry, turning frequently. When cooked, add to the dish and place in a cool oven. Melt a little more butter (or use oil) in the frying pan, add the rice. Stir well until browned, then pour in some of the hot chicken stock. Stirring frequently, cook until the stock has been absorbed, then add more. Do this until all the stock has been added, by which time the rice should be cooked through. Take the dish from the oven, add the contents to the rice in the pan and stir all together, seasoning with salt and black pepper. Return to the hot dish to serve.

This dish may be varied as you like. Pineapple, skinned tomatoes, peas, beans, sprigs of lightly cooked broccoli, etc, can be added and a spoonful or two of soy sauce if liked.

Chicken Tarragon

- 3lb roasting chicken
- 2 rounded teasps dried tarragon
- salt and pepper
- 2oz butter
- 2 medium carrots
- 2 medium onions
- 1¼ pints stock (with a cube)
- 2 tbsp sherry
- 1½ teasp cornflour

Set oven to Mark 4. Wipe the chicken. Put 1 teasp tarragon and salt and pepper inside the bird. Melt the butter in a roasting tin. Peel and thinly slice the carrots and onions and put them in the tin. Put the chicken on top of the vegetables. Cover with foil and cook for 20 mins in the centre of the oven. Take from the oven, remove the foil and pour in the stock. Cover with foil again, return to the oven, put heat to Mark 6. Cook for another hour or until tender. Put the chicken on a hot dish. Strain the liquid from it into a saucepan. Add the rest of the tarragon and sherry. Bring to the boil. Mix the cornflour with a little cold water and stir into the sauce. Season with salt and pepper. Pour a little sauce over the chicken, serve the rest in a jug. Serve with rice.

Chilli Con Carne

* Half – ¾ lb minced lean beef
* 1 large onion
* 1 x 14oz and 1 x 8oz can tomatoes
* 1 bay leaf
* Half – 1 level tablespoon chilli powder
* 1 small teaspoon salt
* Eighth teaspoon cayenne pepper
* Eighth teaspoon paprika
* 1 x 16oz can baked beans

Cook the minced beef in a fairly large pan using a very little fat, until beginning to brown. Add the finely chopped onion and cook for 5 minutes. Add the entire contents of the two tins of tomatoes and all the seasonings. Bring to the boil, cover and simmer gently for 1-2 hours. Add the beans for the last 20 minutes of cooking. If liked, 3 or 4ozs red kidney beans (soaked overnight and simmered in salted water for about ½ – ¾ hour) may be also stirred in at this point. Remove bay leaf before serving.

Cod Baked with Peppers and Onions (Miss Brewster's Cod Bake)

* 1 x 14oz pack frozen cod steaks
* 1 green pepper
* 1 large onion
* 4oz mushrooms
* 1oz butter
* 1oz flour
* ¾ pint of boiling water
* 1 chicken stock cube
* Juice of 1 lemon
* Salt & pepper
* 4 firm tomatoes

Cut the fish into 1-inch cubes, slice the pepper, peel then thinly slice the onion, wash the mushrooms and slice if large, leave whole if small. Place all these in a 2-3 pint oven dish. Melt the butter, add the flour and gradually stir in the boiling water and chicken cube. Stir and bring to the boil, then add the lemon juice and seasoning. Pour over the ingredients in the casserole, cover, and cook at Mark 5 for 50 minutes. After about 30 minutes add the tomatoes, cut into quarters, to the dish. Serve with plain boiled rice.

Cottage Pie

Melt a little fat in a saucepan. Gently cook in it 1 medium onion, sliced and ¾–1lb of lean mined beef. After about 4 minutes stir in the contents of a small tin of tomatoes, 1 level teaspoon salt, a good sprinkling of pepper, a level or small teaspoon of beef extract and quarter – third pint of water depending on the amount of meat. Add a finely-diced carrot. Blend 1 level tablespoon cornflour with a little extra cold water and stir into the mince. Bring to the boil, stirring. Cover and simmer gently for about 30-45 minutes. Place in an ovenproof dish (2 pint size).

Boil 2lbs potatoes in salted water, drain well and dry over a low heat for a few minutes. Mash well, add a little milk, butter, salt and pepper and beat until fluffy. Pile on top of the mince, roughen the top surface and brush with beaten egg. Cook in the centre of a pre-heated oven (Mark 5) for about 25 minutes, when it should be golden brown and crisp. Serve with a green vegetable.

Creamy Malaysian Curry

- ½ oz butter
- 1 onion
- 2 red eating apples
- 3oz sultanas
- Clove of garlic
- 1 large tin Carnation milk
- Curry paste (mild)
- 8-12ozs cooked chicken or turkey pieces
- Coriander or parsley

Melt the butter in a pan. Add the sliced onion and the sliced apples, the sultanas and the crushed garlic. Cook over a gentle heat until softened, then transfer to a bowl. Add the Carnation milk to the pan, reserving a little to blend in with 2 tablespoons of plain flour and add this too. Bring to the boil, stirring continuously until thickened. Blend in 4 tablespoons of chicken or turkey stock and 6 teaspoons of the curry paste. Add the softened fruit mixture and the chicken or turkey pieces (or prawns could be used). Heat gently to warm all the ingredients and serve on a bed of rice garnished with the coriander or parsley.

Devilled Chicken Breasts

* Marinade:
* 2 tablespoons Worcester sauce
* 1 tablespoon tomato puree
* 3 tablespoons oil
* 1 crushed garlic clove
* 2 tablespoons paprika
* 2 teaspoons ground ginger
* 2 teaspoons turmeric
* 2 teaspoons salt
* 4 chicken breasts, skinned

Place the chicken in a shallow dish, combine the marinade ingredients. Pour over the chicken, cover and chill for 2-4 hours, turning occasionally. Place under a moderate grill and cook for about 20 minutes. Baste with the marinade and turn occasionally until the chicken is cooked. Serve with lemon wedges and a salad or rice.

Devilled Haddock

- 12oz fresh haddock
- 1oz butter
- A small bay leaf
- Salt & pepper
- ½ oz flour
- ¼ pint milk
- ½ teasp anchovy essence
- 1 teasp Worcester sauce
- 1 teasp mango chutney
- ½ level teasp dry mustard
- A pinch of cayenne

Set the oven to Mark 4. Wash the fish and cut into portions. Butter an ovenproof dish and put the fish into it with the bay leaf. Season and pour in ¼ pint cold water. Cover with a lid or foil. Cook in the centre of the oven for 20 minutes. Melt about 1.2 oz butter in a pan and add the flour. Cook gently for 2 minutes, then take off heat. Gradually add milk. Return to the heat, bring to the boil stirring all the time. Simmer for 2 mins and season. Mix the anchovy essence with the Worcester sauce, chutney, mustard and cayenne. Stir this mixture with the sauce, pour over the fish and serve hot.

Fish Cakes

Use 2 steaks of fresh haddock. Cook these in milk with seasonings and a bay leaf (if liked) in a covered dish at Gas No. 4 for about 30 minutes. Boil a good-sized potato, or 2 small ones, peeled and cut up, until tender then mash well with butter and a good shake of black pepper. Flake the cooked fish, add to the potato and pound well together. Also add a little chopped fresh parsley or dried parsley. Form into small cakes (about 8) roll in the milk in which the fish was cooked and coat with seasoned flour or breadcrumbs. Chill before frying.

Fish Moussaka

- 1 lb cod fillet
- Half lb tomatoes
- Half lb onions
- Three quarter lb aubergines
- Three quarter pint milk
- 1½ ozs butter
- 1 oz plain flour
- 1 egg (large)
- Salt and pepper
- 6 tablespoons cooking oil
- 1 oz dried white breadcrumbs

Slice the aubergines slantwise fairly thinly, lay on a plate and sprinkle with salt. Skin the fillet and place in a greased 3 pint oven dish. Peel and slice the tomatoes and onions. Place the tomatoes on top of the fish. Cover with the breadcrumbs. Dry the aubergine slices with soft paper and fry in the oil until light brown on both sides. Put on top of the breadcrumbs. Fry the onions in the butter until soft but not brown. Stir in the flour, mix till smooth. Gradually add the milk, stir until boiling, then simmer for a few moments. Season. Separate the egg, beat the yolk into the sauce. Whisk the white until very stiff, fold into the sauce. Pour into the dish, bake at Mark 4, centre shelf, for about 45 minutes. Serve with rolls and butter.

Gammon Toppers

* 4 slices gammon
* 1 cooking apple
* Juice of half a lemon
* 1 teaspoon flour
* 1 teaspoon paprika pepper
* Quarter pint milk
* 2 teaspoons sieved tomato
* Pinch of sugar

Place the slices of gammon (fairly thick) in a casserole. Peel, core and slice the apple into rings, place on top of the rashers and add the lemon juice. Brush with oil or melted butter and bake at Mark 5 for 20 minutes. Mix the flour and paprika with the tomato puree and sugar, add the milk and mix to a smooth paste. Cook until thick and serve poured over the rashers.

Haddock en Croute

* 13oz pack puff pastry (frozen)
* 4 haddock steaks (frozen)
* 2-4ozs mushrooms

Roll the pastry to a rectangle 14" x 16", trim the edges. Place the steaks on the pastry 1½ inches apart. Wash and slice the mushrooms and sprinkle over each steak. Season well. Wrap the pastry over to form a long parcel, seal the edges and ends well and turn over so that the joins are underneath. Mark a division between each steak with the side of the hand and put a pastry diamond (made from the trimmings) on top of each. Brush with beaten egg and bake in the centre of the oven, mark 7 for 10 minutes, then at mark 5 for a further 30 minutes.

Hotpot

Trim the surplus fat from about 1½–2lbs of middle neck of lamb chops. Into the bottom of a deep casserole put 2 or 3 smallish potatoes sliced into rings, half of a large onion finely sliced, 3 or 4 whole pickling onions and a sliced carrot. Place half the lamb pieces on these vegetables, season with salt, pepper and a little sage or herbs, then cover with another layer of potato slices, the other half of the onion, also sliced, 3 or 4 more pickling onions, another carrot and then the remaining lamb. Again season with salt, pepper, sage or herbs and cover with a final good layer of sliced potatoes. Season lightly, and pour about a pint of good chicken stock (made with a cube) into the dish. Vegetable water, left-over gravy etc may be used at this point. Cover the dish and cook for about 3 hours at Mark 3. Uncover the dish to allow the potatoes to brown during the last 20-30 minutes.

Kedgeree

Take a good piece of smoked cod or haddock (about ½ – ¾ lbs) and poach gently in water. Melt about 1oz of butter in a saucepan, stir in 1 or 2 teaspoons of curry powder. Add a medium sized chopped onion and 2 chopped garlic cloves, and cook for a few minutes.+ Then add 10 fluid ounces of long grain rice, stir well and cook while stirring until the rice is browned. Pour on 1 pint of water, using the water in which the fish was poached.* Simmer. Remove the skin and bones from the fish and flake, not too finely. When the rice is cooked drain well, add a good knob of butter and fold through. Add the flaked fish, then 1 or 2 chopped hard boiled eggs, reserving a little for garnish and also a little chopped parsley if you have it. Sprinkle with cayenne pepper.

+ Add 2-4ozs mushrooms
* Add salt, or try a fish stock cube. Pilau rice cube is good.

Marjorie's Galantine
(Marjorie's recipe)

Take 2lbs of rump steak and three quarters of a pound of raw ham. Process in a blender or chop finely. Add seasonings of salt and pepper, thyme, rosemary, mace and parsley. I suggest a small teaspoon of salt, half teaspoon of pepper, half teaspoon of each of the herbs and 2 teaspoons of parsley. Mix well, add a beaten egg and stir all together. Turn into a buttered terrine, cover with a buttered paper and a foil lid, well sealed down. Place the terrine in a baking tin with water to come well up the sides and bake in the oven, gas mark 4/5 for about 2 hours.

Meat & Vegetable Pie

Take 6-8ozs lean minced beef and place in a saucepan with a finely-sliced onion. Add a diced carrot, a diced potato, and small amounts of any other suitable vegetables you may have – such as a stick of celery (chopped), turnip, swede, parsnip, leek, etc. Cover with water, bring to simmering point, add seasoning and a bay leaf. Simmer very gently for 1-1½ hours. Allow to cool. Line a plate with short pastry, and put into it the meat and vegetables, being careful not to add too much liquid – just enough to keep the filling nice and moist. Cover with pastry, brush over with milk and bake for about half hour at Mark 5, on shelf above centre. Serve with potatoes (jacket-baked or mashed) and a green vegetable. Any liquid reserved from the filling should be heated and served separately.

Mediterranean Lamb

- ✳ 2 level tbsp. chopped parsley
- ✳ 1½ tbsp. dried rosemary
- ✳ ½ level teasp. garlic salt
- ✳ 2 tbsp corn oil
- ✳ 2lb piece leg of lamb
- ✳ ¾ pint chicken stock (with a cube)
- ✳ 2 medium tomatoes
- ✳ 5oz pkt. frozen peas
- ✳ 1 dessertsp. anchovy essence
- ✳ ground black pepper

Set oven to Mark 4. Mix parsley with rosemary, garlic and 1 tbsp oil. With a sharp knife cut surface of meat into a diamond pattern. Spread herb mixture over the meat. Put in roasting tin, add stock. Cook (covered) in centre of oven for 1½-2 hours, basting often. Cut tomatoes in half, brush with oil. Put in ovenproof dish, cook in the oven for 10 mins. Cook the peas. Put the meat on a hot dish, mix anchovy essence with meat sauce, season with pepper. Simmer until slightly thickened.

Pot Roast of Pheasant with Shallots

Adapted from a Delia Smith recipe.

- ✳ 2 pheasants
- ✳ Red wine
- ✳ Brandy
- ✳ 12 shallots
- ✳ 6ozs mushrooms (approx).

Melt an ounce of butter and a tablespoon of oil in a heavy frying pan and brown the pheasants until they are a golden colour all over. Place them breast uppermost in a deep casserole, season well. Brown the shallots in the frying pan and the washed and sliced mushrooms. Put 3 tablespoons of brandy into a pan, heat and ignite. Carefully pour the flaming brandy over the pheasants. Make a pint of stock, using the drained blood of the pheasants, vegetable liquor, a stock cube or whatever, and add to the mushrooms and shallots in the frying pan. Bring to simmering point, simmer gently and add half pint of red wine. Pour over the pheasants, season well, add 2 bay leaves and sprigs of thyme. Cover well and simmer for 1½ – 2 hours very gently on the top of the stove. Thicken the sauce with a mixed flour and butter paste.

Plate Meat Pie

I took around three quarters lb of lean rump steak, removed all fat, skin etc and gave it a few seconds in the Magimix (having first cut it into fairly small chunks). I halved a medium onion, sliced it thinly (just one half) and fried in butter (or oil) until golden. I put these aside and fried in the pan about 6 medium mushrooms, having first rinsed them and cut into slices. I added the fried onion and mushrooms to the prepared meat and stirred all together, adding seasonings – salt, pepper, herbs of choice, etc – and finally a little stock for moisture. I prepared 8ozs of short-crust pastry and lined my blue enamel plate with half of it, rolled out fairly thinly. I added the meat filling, evenly spread, and topped with the remaining pastry. I spread the pie with a little beaten egg and baked at Gas no 6 for about 30 minutes, then as Gas No 4 for a further 20 minutes or so.

Pork and Bean Dinner

- ✳ 1 aubergine
- ✳ 2 tablespoons oil
- ✳ 2 small onions
- ✳ 1 green pepper
- ✳ 4ozs mushrooms
- ✳ ¼ pint beef stock or water
- ✳ 4 tablespoons tomato ketchup
- ✳ 1 tablespoon distilled vinegar
- ✳ ½ teaspoon salt, some black pepper
- ✳ ½ teaspoon oregano
- ✳ 15oz can Heinz beans
- ✳ 4-6 lean pork chops

Chop the aubergine, sprinkle with salt and leave to stand for 20 minutes, then rinse and dry well. Gently fry the sliced onions, aubergine, strips of green pepper and quartered mushrooms until the onions are lightly browned. Add the stock, ketchup, vinegar and seasonings. Bring to the boil. Cover the pan, lower the heat and simmer for 10 minutes. Add the beans to the sauce after 8 minutes. Pre-heat the oven to mark 4. Fry or grill the chops lightly to seal in the juices. Place the sauce in a shallow casserole. Place the chops on top, cover with a lid or foil and bake for about 1 hour. Garnish with apple or onion rings.

Pork Chops with Orange & Thyme

- ✳ 2 lean pork chops
- ✳ Salt and pepper
- ✳ 1oz butter
- ✳ 4 lumps sugar
- ✳ 3 tbsp vinegar
- ✳ 2 small oranges
- ✳ ¼ level teasp dried thyme

Season the chops with salt and pepper. Fry in butter for 6-7 minutes on both sides or until well cooked. Reserve the juices. Put the sugar and vinegar in a small pan and heat gently until melted. Boil until the mixture is a rich brown. Pour the reserved juices into it. Put half an orange aside. Squeeze the juice from the rest and add to the sugar mixture with the thyme. Bring to the boil. Put the chops on to a hot serving dish. Pour the sauce over them, and use the remaining half-orange for garnish.

Porterhouse Steaks

Good rump steak may also be cooked in this way.

Peel and slice two large onions and fry in a very little fat until soft and golden. Place in a shallow dish and put in a warm place. Add an ounce or two of butter to the frying-pan and place the steaks (previously trimmed and seasoned) in the hot butter. Fry for 5-10 minutes on each side, quickly at first to brown and then more slowly. When cooked, place on the onions. Add a little stock, wine or water to the frying-pan and boil up gently, stirring well to incorporate the sediments and juices from the pan. Pour over the steaks and serve immediately with vegetables.

Pot Roast of Beef

I bought a piece of rolled brisket (from Waitrose) weighing nearly 2lbs. I used this recipe:

I wiped the meat and rolled it in seasoned flour. I browned it on all sides in hot dripping and took it from the pan. I peeled and sliced 2 onions, 2 carrots, half turnip, and 2 or 3 green sticks of celery and added these vegetables to the hot fat. I let them brown lightly, then replaced the meat on top. I added seasonings, bouquet garni and stock, enough to cover the vegetables (I find it wise to be generous, the liquid is important) and covered the pan. I simmered it gently, allowing about 40 minutes to the pound and 30 minutes over. It may be necessary to add extra stock during this time. When cooked, I lifted the meat onto a hot plate and served the vegetables, using the liquid for gravy.

Potted Meat
(Mrs. Duckworth's* recipe)

* 1lb carrots
* 1 medium onion
* 1 potato (about 6ozs)
* 2ozs butter
* 2 pints chicken stock*
* Half teaspoon thyme or a bouquet garni
* Quarter pint single cream
* Small teaspoon sugar

Peel and thinly slice the carrots and onion. Melt the butter in a large saucepan, add the vegetables and fry gently, with the pan covered, for about 10 minutes, until they are soft but not brown. Pour in the stock, then add the potato, peeled and diced. Add the thyme or bouquet garni and seasonings and sugar. Stir well and bring to simmering point. Cook gently for about 1 hour. Sieve, return to the pan and re-heat, then stir in the cream. Check the seasonings and serve very hot but do not allow to boil after the cream has been added.

I think that rather than sieve all the soup, I would sieve about one third and then add to the remainder. The texture is better and the flavour very good. Some finely-sliced celery green is a good addition to the vegetables.

*Marjorie's mother-in-law

Provençal Beef Casserole

- ✴ Half lb mushrooms
- ✴ 1 onion
- ✴ 1 pint of stock
- ✴ 1oz of butter

Trim 1-1½ lbs good stewing steak (shoulder, buttock or topside) and some lambs' kidney. Coat in seasoned flour, fry briefly then remove from pan. Fry 2-3 crushed garlic cloves and 2-3 sliced onions until soft, put into a casserole, add the meat, a small tin of sweet red peppers (sliced), quarter pound sliced mushrooms, tinned tomatoes (drained, a medium tin). Make a gravy in the pan used for frying, using half pint of stock and the liquor from the can of tomatoes. Add a little tomato puree. Pour over the casserole contents, season well and add oregano and paprika. Cook for 1 hour at Mark 3, then 2 hours at Mark 2. Stir in 2 or 3 tablespoons of single cream or soured cream before serving. Check the seasoning.

Salmis of Pheasant

Roast the pheasant for 20-30 minutes, cut into neat joints and remove the skin. Place the joints in a flameproof casserole. Take about 1oz butter and a little oil and heat until sizzling. Add a small sliced onion, a stalk of chopped celery, an ounce or so of sliced mushrooms and a small sliced carrot. Fry gently until golden (about 10 minutes). Stir in a tablespoon (about 1 oz) of flour and cook, stirring, until it turns light brown. Gradually blend in about half a pint of beef stock, to which add the reserved blood of the pheasant, and about a quarter pint of red wine. Cook, stirring, until it comes to the boil, thickened and smooth. Add 1 level dessertspoon of redcurrant jelly. Pour this over the pheasant. Cover and simmer very gently for about 30 minutes, add 6ozs button mushrooms and simmer for about a further 20 minutes, or until the pheasant is tender.

Salmon Quiche

* 2 tablespoons minced shallots
* 1½ ozs butter
* 4ozs sliced mushrooms
* 4ozs flaked salmon
* Salt & pepper
* 2 tablespoons Madeira or white vermouth

* 3 eggs
* 8ozs thick cream
* 1 tablespoon tomato paste
* Parsley or dill
* 2ozs Swiss cheese, grated
* 1 10-inch pastry flan case, part cooked

Fry the shallots in butter until transparent. Add the mushrooms, cook for 1-2 minutes. Add salmon, seasonings and wine. Cook for 2-3 minutes, then set aside to cook a little. Beat the eggs, cream, tomato paste and chopped parsley or dill. Add the egg mixture to the first mixture. Put into the pastry shell, scatter cheese on top. Bake at gas mark 5-6 for about 30 minutes, until puffy and brown.

Salmon & Sweetcorn Pie

* 1¼ lb potatoes, peeled
* 1 tablespoon oil
* 1 red or green pepper, diced
* Half pint well-seasoned white saucepan

* 198g can of sweetcorn, drained
* 212g can red salmon, drained
* 2ozs cheddar cheese, grated

Boil the potatoes. Meanwhile, heat the oil in a pan and fry the pepper for a minute or so. Bring the white sauce to the boil and add the pepper, then simmer for 1-2 minutes. Remove from the heat and add the sweetcorn and salmon. Put into a flameproof dish. Drain the potatoes and slice over the salmon mixture. Top with the cheese and grill until golden.

Seafarer's Rice

* ½ lb fresh white haddock
* ½ lb smoked haddock
* 6ozs long grain rice
* ½ lb frozen mixed vegetables
* 4ozs shrimps or prawns

Skin the fish and cut into cubes. Poach for about 15-20 minutes in about ¾ pint of water with the juice of half a lemon. Cook the rice in boiling salted water for about 8 minutes, then add the mixed vegetables. Continue cooking for a further 10 minutes, drain well. Place in a dish, put the fish on top and cat with a sauce made from butter, flour, milk, seasonings and the shrimps or prawns.

Spaghetti Bolognese

- ✸ 12 ozs spaghetti
- ✸ 1 ½ tablespoons tomato puree
- ✸ ½ lb peeled tomatoes or tinned tomatoes
- ✸ ½ lb lean minced beef
- ✸ 1 onion
- ✸ 2 tablespoons olive oil
- ✸ 1oz butter
- ✸ 1 bay leaf

Chop onion finely and fry until tender in olive oil and butter. Add the minced beef and allow to brown slightly before adding the tomatoes and tomato puree and the bay leaf. Allow to simmer for about 1 hour. Boil the spaghetti for 10 minutes in salt water. Test to ensure not overcooked. Place spaghetti in a dish, pour the sauce over and stir in.

Spiced Beef

- 3-3½ lb piece of topside or silverside
- Marinade
- Quarter pint red wine
- Quarter pint wine vinegar
- Half pint water
- 1 medium onion, sliced
- 2 tablespoons soft brown sugar
- Bouquet Garni
- Pinch of thyme

Put the meat into a deep dish. Mix the ingredients for the marinade and pour over the meat. Put (covered) into the refrigerator, and leave overnight.

Melt 2ozs butter in a thick pan, wipe the meat with absorbent paper and brown evenly in the hot fat. Put in a baking tin, pour the marinade over and cook at Mark 3 for 3-3½ hours. Drain off the liquid. Put a small amount into a basin and add 1oz flour. Mix to a smooth paste. Heat the remainder, stir in the flour mixture, and cook and stir until boiling. Stir in quarter pint sour cream and serve with the meat.

Spiced Pickled Beef

- ☀ 4lbs silverside of beef
- ☀ 2 onions
- ☀ 1 inch piece of root ginger
- ☀ 8ozs coarse sea salt
- ☀ 2 teaspoons ground black pepper
- ☀ 1 teaspoon cayenne
- ☀ 1 teaspoon cloves
- ☀ 10 juniper berries
- ☀ 1 teaspoon allspice
- ☀ 5ozs soft dark brown sugar

Peel and thinly slice the carrots and onion. Melt the butter in a large saucepan, add the vegetables and fry gently, with the pan covered, for about 10 minutes, until they are soft but not brown. Pour in the stock, then add the potato, peeled and diced. Add the thyme or bouquet garni and seasonings and sugar. Stir well and bring to simmering point. Cook gently for about 1 hour. Sieve, return to the pan and re-heat, then stir in the cream. Check the seasonings and serve very hot but do not allow to boil after the cream has been added.

I think that rather than sieve all the soup, I would sieve about one third and then add to the remainder. The texture is better and the flavour very good. Some finely-sliced celery green is a good addition to the vegetables.

Spicy Sardines in Tomato Sauce

Heat a little oil in a frying pan. Fry 1 crushed clove of garlic, 2 finely-chopped sticks of celery and I finely-chopped small white onion for about 10 minutes. Add 1 tablespoon tomato puree, I teaspoon chilli powder and 6 ripe chopped tomatoes (skinned). Heat a little oil in a frying pan and add 6-8 fresh sardines, tails removed. Simmer the sauce for about 10 minutes (covered) and cook the sardines over a gentle heat for about 10 minutes, turning occasionally. Add the tomato sauce and cook, covered for a further 5 minutes. Serve with crusty bread.

Spicy Lasagne

Bolognese Sauce

- 2ozs olive oil
- 2 onions, peeled and chopped
- 2ozs bacon (unsmoked)
- 1lb minced beef
- 5ozs tomato paste
- 14oz can tomatoes
- 1 teaspoon oregano
- Seasonings

Cheese Sauce

- 1½ ozs butter
- 1½ ozs plain flour
- 1 pint milk
- 3ozs grated cheddar cheese
- 2 teaspoons prepared French mustard
- Salt and pepper
- Olive oil
- 6ozs lasagne verde

To make the Bolognese sauce, heat the oil in a saucepan. Gently fry the onions and finely diced bacon until softened. Add the beef and cook until just browned. Drain off the fat. Reduce the heat and stir in the tomato paste and canned tomatoes. Season to taste. Cover and simmer for 40 minutes. Add the oregano.

Now make the cheese sauce. Melt the butter in a saucepan. Stir in the flour and cook for a minute or two. Remove from the heat and gradually stir in the milk. Cook, stirring until thick. Add half the cheese and the mustard and season to taste.

Cook the lasagne in plenty of boiling salted water to which 1 teaspoon of oil has been added. Cook for 10 minutes or until just soft. Drain in a colander. Rinse well, then drain on kitchen paper. Grease an oven dish and line with a third of the lasagne. Top with half the meat sauce and one third of the cheese sauce. Cover with half the remaining, the rest of the meat sauce and half the remaining cheese sauce. Sprinkle with the rest of the cheese, cook at mark 4 for about 40 minutes.

Steak & Kidney Pie (1)

Trim 2lbs lean shoulder steak and 2 lambs' kidneys. Cut into small pieces and coat well with seasoned flour. Pack into a pie dish so that it is well-filled and add a small onion finely sliced. Pour over sufficient stock (made with a chicken or beef cube) almost to fill the dish, cover closely with foil and cook at Mark 2 for 2 hours. Remove from the oven and allow to cool for a few minutes. Then take off the foil and cover with a lid of short or flaky pastry, using a pie-funnel. Brush with egg yolk and bake at Mark 5 for about 30 minutes.

Steak & Kidney Pie (2)

Trim 1lb lean shoulder steak free from all gristle and fat and cut into small pieces (or mince) Add one or two sliced lamb's kidneys and put into seasoned flour with the meat. Coat well, place into a saucepan, add a chopped small onion, cover with stock or water and simmer very gently for 1 and half to 2 hours. Allow to cool. Line a plate with shortcrust pastry, pour into it the meat filling, season well, place a pastry lid on top and brush with milk. Bake for about half to ¾ hour at Gas Mark 5.

Stir-Fry

- 1 large onion
- 8ozs potatoes
- 4ozs cabbage (or iceberg lettuce)
- 2 or 3 tomatoes
- 4ozs mushrooms
- 6 frankfurters or similar sausage

This is especially good if new potatoes are used.

Heat a little oil and an ounce or two of butter in a large frying pan. Peel and finely chop the onion and put it into the pan, together with the potatoes, which should have been boiled for about 10-15 minutes, then add the cabbage (or lettuce), the skinned and sliced tomatoes and the sliced mushrooms. Season well and fry for about a further 10 minutes. Finally add the sliced frankfurters, fry for a few more minutes and serve.

Stuffed Marrow Rings

- 1 marrow
- 4ozs chopped mushrooms
- 4ozs chopped bacon
- 2ozs cooked rice
- 1 teaspoon chopped parsley
- 1 teaspoon rubbed sage
- 2ozs cheddar cheese
- Beaten egg
- Salt and pepper

For a stronger flavour Parmesan cheese could be used.

Peel the marrow and cut into 4 sections. Remove the seeds and fibres from the centre. Mix the remaining ingredients together except for 1oz of the cheese.
Place the marrow rings in an ovenproof dish, stuff with the mushroom mixture. Bake at Gas No 5 for 45 minutes. Sprinkle with the remaining cheese before serving.

Sweet & Sour Sausages

- 1 green pepper
- 2 rings tinned pineapple
- 1 medium onion
- half oz margarine
- 2 rounded teaspoons cornflour
- 2 tablespoons pineapple syrup
- 2-3 teaspoons chutney
- 3 level teaspoons tomato puree
- 2 teaspoons soy sauce
- 2 level teaspoons caster sugar
- 1 tablespoon vinegar
- half pint water
- 8oz can hot-dog sausages
- 6-8ozs long grain rice.

Slice the pepper into strips, discarding the seeds, core and white pith. Place in a small saucepan, cover with cold water and bring to the boil. Simmer for 3 minutes, then drain. Cut pineapple into pieces, add to the pepper. Peel and slice the onion. Melt the margarine in a medium saucepan, add the onion and cook without browning for 3 minutes. Stir in the cornflour, pineapple syrup, chutney, tomato puree, soy sauce, sugar, vinegar, and water. Bring to the boil, stirring. Drain the sausages and cut into slices. Add to the sauce and simmer for 10 minutes. Add the pineapple and green pepper and simmer for a further five minutes. Serve with cooked rice.

Tagliatelle in Cream Sauce

- 8ozs mushrooms
- 10oz butter
- Lemon juice
- 4ozs cooked ham
- ½ pint double cream
- Salt & black pepper
- Grated nutmeg
- 1 tablespoon stock
- 2 – 3ozs grated cheese (Parmesan or Cheddar)

Slice the mushrooms finely and cook in the butter and a good squeeze of lemon juice until just softened. Add the ham cut into fine strips, the cream, seasonings, pinch of nutmeg, stock and 1 tablespoon cheese. Stir well, bring to the boil and simmer gently while cooking the tagliatelle. When this is cooked, drain well and pour into a heated serving dish. Pour on half the cream mixture and mix in well. Pour the rest of the cream mixture over the top. Serve with the remaining cheese.

Tomato Casserole

- 1½ lbs lean stewing steak
- 1 tablespoon oil
- 2 medium onions
- 15oz can of tomatoes
- 2 tablespoons tomato ketchup
- 1 teaspoon caster sugar
- Bouquet garni
- ¼ pint water
- 4oz small mushrooms
- 1 tablespoon flour

Cut the meat into small cubes. Fry for a couple of minutes in the oil, place in a casserole. Slice the onions, fry for about 5 minutes. Add to the casserole. Blend together the tomatoes, tomato ketchup, sugar, bouquet garni and half the water. Pour over the meat. Cook at mark 3 for about 2½ hours. About an hour before the end of the cooking time, add the trimmed mushrooms. Blend the flour with the remaining water and stir this into the casserole also. Return to the oven for the remainder of the time. Remove the bouquet garni before serving.

Tuna Fish Cakes

Use salmon instead of tuna if preferred.

- ✳ 8oz tin of tuna fish
- ✳ 4 small potatoes
- ✳ 1 egg
- ✳ Chopped parsley

Boil the potatoes until tender, mash very thoroughly with a good piece of butter. Mix with the flaked tuna fish and chopped parsley and work well together, seasoning well. Add a little beaten egg, bind smoothly together and form into small cakes. Coat each with a little flour, brush with beaten egg and roll in fresh white breadcrumbs. Chill for a time before frying until golden brown.

Tuna Savoury

Melt 2 ozs butter in a pan, fry a chopped onion in it for 5 minutes. Add a tablespoon of tomato puree, a 14 oz can of tomatoes, quarter teaspoon of basil and seasonings. Take a 7 oz can of tuna fish and flake the contents, then add the sauce. Cook 8 ozs of macaroni or spaghetti in boiling salted water, turn into a serving dish, and pour the hot tuna sauce over. Sprinkle with grated cheese. 2-4 ozs mushrooms can be fried with the onion, or fried separately and stirred into the sauce before serving.

Two Pheasants

Chris gave me 2 pheasants, a cock and a hen. I washed them thoroughly. I melted an ounce or two of butter (or butter and groundnut oil) in my FE casserole and browned the pheasants all over. I put them aside and browned a dozen shallots and some sliced celery (you could add other vegetables if wanted). I removed these and replaced the pheasants. I heated 3 tablespoons of brandy, set it alight and poured it flaming over the birds (be careful). I added the vegetables, seasoned it all well and poured in half pint beef stock, 1 glass of port, the blood of the pheasants and then a little extra stock and a couple of bay leaves. I covered the casserole with foil and a lid and simmered very gently for 1½ ours. After the birds and the vegetables were lifted to warm plates and dishes I mixed one teaspoon of flour with 1 teaspoon of softened butter to a smooth cream and beat (with a balloon whisk) into the gravy to give it more body. The liquid seemed much reduced in the cooking, I was glad of a little extra stock to add to it.

Sauces, Vegetables and Miscellaneous

Cumberland Sauce

* 8 fluid ozs red wine
* ¾ lb redcurrant jelly
* 1 lemon, grated rind and juice
* 1 orange, grated rind and juice
* 1 rounded teaspoon cornflour
* 1 dessertspoon sugar

Boil the wine rapidly until reduced by half. Add the redcurrant jelly with the orange and lemon rind and juice. Stir over a gentle heat until the jelly is melted. Blend the cornflour to a smooth paste with 1 tablespoon water and stir into the sauce. Bring to the boil, simmer gently for 5 minutes until slightly thickened, add the sugar (to taste). Serve with ham, pork, sausages, etc.

Celeriac

I bought a fairly large root but forgot to weigh it. I peeled it thickly, the outside being very knobbly and hard. I washed it and cut it into several pieces, rather like pre-preparing potatoes for roasting. I heated some dripping (or you could use oil or butter) in a roasting pan. I put the celeriac pieces into a pan and covered them with boiling water. I simmered them for about 5 minutes, then drained them well. I seasoned them with a shake of pepper and salt, then rolled them in seasoned flour. I put them in the hot dripping in the roasting pan and cooked them at Gas No 5 for about an hour, turning them from time to time.

Dallas's*
Salad Dressing

Take 2 tablespoons of extra virgin olive oil and add 1 tablespoon of wine vinegar. Shake well in a covered jar, then add a squeeze or two of lemon juice, a shake of salt and black pepper and about quarter to half teaspoon of made mustard, ad also a sprinkle of caster sugar. Shake very well together and serve.

Mum's younger sister

Devilled
Beans

(good with pork chops, bacon or sausages)

Empty a large can of baked beans into an ovenproof dish. Stir in 1 teaspoon made mustard, 1-2 teaspoons Worcester sauce, 1 teaspoon brown sugar and a sprinkle of cayenne pepper. Heat through, with the dish covered, in a moderate oven.

Forcemeat Stuffing for a Small Turkey

- 6ozs white breadcrumbs
- 3 tablespoons flaked suet
- Small bunch of parsley
- 1 teaspoon mixed herbs
- The meat of 1 sausage (if available)
- 1 shallot or small piece of a large onion
- 1 egg
- Seasonings

Mix the breadcrumbs, suet, herbs, seasonings, finely-chopped onion and finely-chopped parsley. Add the sausage meat and bind to a soft mixture with the beaten egg.

Hot Devilled Potato Salad

* 1lb new potatoes or 1 x 15oz can new potatoes
* Salt
* Quarter pint double cream
* 1 tablespoon fresh chopped parsley or chives
* Pepper
* 2 tablespoons Worcester sauce

Scrape, boil and drain the potatoes or heat up the can. Combine cream, Worcester sauce and parsley or chives. Slice the potatoes and mix while hot with the cream mixture. Season well. Serve with steaks, chops, chicken or fish.

New Potatoes

It seems now to be possible to buy various kinds of new potatoes during most of the year. They seem to come from all parts of the world – Spain, Italy, France or wherever. Quite often they are very small.

I find that the nicest way to cook them is to cover them with cold water, bring to the boil and simmer for about 15 minutes. Pour off the water and cover with cold water. When the potatoes are cool enough to handle, skin them (easy but a bit messy), rinse and place in the pan again. Cover with boiling water, add salt and a sprig or two of mint (or mint stalks if the leaves have dried off). Bring slowly back to simmering point, cook a further 10-15 minutes, drain and serve buttered.

Chris says that cooked this way, they taste exactly like Jersey new potatoes.

Oven-Roasted Broccoli Florets

* Half lb mushrooms
* 1 onion
* 1 pint of stock
* 1oz of butter

* Half lb mushrooms
* 1 onion
* 1 pint of stock
* 1oz of butter

Wipe and slice the mushrooms and chop the onion. Melt the butter in a fairly large saucepan and sauté the mushrooms and onion for about 2-3 minutes until soft. Pour in the stock. Blend the flour with a little of the milk and add gradually to the soup with the rest of the milk. Season to taste. Bring to the boil stirring all the while and then simmer gently for three quarters – 1 hour.

Stuffing for Mackerel, trout, etc.

Breadcrumbs, good pinch mixed herbs, chopped parsley, 3-4 ozs chopped lightly fried mushrooms, 1-2 skinned chopped tomatoes, seasonings. Bind with beaten egg.

Cakes and Puddings

Almond & Lemon Shortbread

- ☀ 4ozs softened butter
- ☀ 2ozs caster sugar
- ☀ ½ teaspoon finely grated lemon zest
- ☀ 2ozs ground almonds
- ☀ 5ozs plain flour
- ☀ ½ oz flaked almonds
- ☀ 1 tablespoon caster sugar

Cream the butter with the sugar and lemon zest until well mixed. Gradually work in the ground almonds and flour until the mixture forms a soft dough that can be shaped into a ball. Divide the dough into two and roll or press each piece into a 6-7" circle, then transfer to a lightly-buttered baking sheet. Sprinkle the flaked almonds over the shortbread and decorate the edges with your fingertips. Mark each round into 6 pieces. Bake at mark 3 for 25-30 minutes. Cool for about 5 minutes on the baking sheet, transfer to a wire rack and sprinkle with the extra sugar. Cut into pieces when cold, carefully.

Almond Squares

- ✹ Puff pastry
- ✹ 2ozs caster sugar
- ✹ 4ozs ground almonds
- ✹ 1 tablespoon desiccated coconut
- ✹ 1oz butter or margarine
- ✹ 2ozs walnuts
- ✹ 1 egg

Roll out the pastry very thinly and line a small baking sheet. Chop the walnuts finely and mix with the coconut. Beat the sugar and butter to a cream, stir in the egg yolk and beat well. Add the ground almonds and chopped nuts and mix well together. Spread this mixture over the pastry and bake at gas no. 4 for about 20 mins. When cooked, brush over the top with a whipped egg white, dredge with caster sugar and coconut and return to the oven to dry and brown lightly. Cut into squares.

Apple and Apricot Slice

Roll a small packet of frozen puff pastry to a rectangle about 13 inches x 5 inches. Peel, core and slice 1lb of small baking apples and arrange the pieces in pairs all down the pastry strip. Drain juice from a small tin of apricot halves and arrange the halves in a row down the centre of the strip. Place an apple slice between each half. Sprinkle the fruit generously with caster sugar. Bake at Mark 7 for 25 minutes, then at Mark 4 for 5-10 minutes. Make a syrup with the apricot juice and arrowroot and spoon over the fruit or use warmed apricot jam thinned down with a little water. Serve with whipped cream.

Apple Cream

* 2lbs cooking apples
* ¼ pint double cream
* Sugar to taste

Peel the apples and cut into small pieces. Stew with the sugar and a little cold water until soft. Cool and pass through a sieve. Whip the cream until thick (but not too stiff) and add to the apples. Whisk together, chill before serving.

Apple Gingerbread

* 8ozs baking apples
* 1 level tablespoon sugar
* 2 tablespoons water
* 4oz golden syrup
* 3oz butter
* 2ozs demerara sugar
* 6ozs SR flour
* 2 level teaspoons ground ginger
* ¼ teaspoon cinnamon
* 1 large egg

Peel, core and slice the apples, stew gently with the sugar and water until tender, then beat to a puree. Leave to cool. Weigh the syrup into a pan, add the demerara sugar and the butter and melt over a gentle heat. Stir in the sieved flour with the spices, then beat in the egg. Lastly, add the cooled apple. Pour into a greased and lined 7 to 8 inch square tin and bake in the centre of the oven, mark 4, for about 1-1¼ hours.

Apples with Apricots

Take 6 dessert apples, peel and core them and tie a 2 inch strip of greased paper round the outside of each. Place on a baking/serving dish, fill the centres of each with caster sugar and 2 tablespoons of chopped dried apricots (ready-to-eat type). Top each apple with a nut of butter and pour 6 tablespoons of sweet white wine into the dish. Bake at mark 4 for about 25-30 minutes. Take from the oven and remove the apples from the dish. Pour the buttery juices into a saucepan and add 1 tablespoon of apricot jam. Sprinkle the top of each apple with a little icing sugar and glaze under the grill. Meanwhile, bring the sauce to simmering point and simmer gently for a few minutes. Pour round the apples and serve.

Apple Meringue Pie

Line a pie-plate with shortcrust pastry. Crimp, or otherwise decorate, the edge and lightly prick the base. Peel and core 2 medium baking apples, slice thinly and place in a saucepan with 2 or 3 tablespoons of sugar and a little water. Stew gently until tender, then leave to cool for a few minutes. Beat with a fork, then beat in the yolk of an egg. Pour this mixture into the pastry-lined plate, dot with a few shavings of butter and bake at Mark 5 for about 15 minutes, when the pastry should be lightly browned. Remove from the oven. Whisk the egg white until stiff, then quickly and lightly fold in 2 tablespoons of caster sugar. Spread this over the apple filling, sealing it well to the edges, and sprinkle a little caster sugar over the top. Return to the oven at Mark 2 and bake for about 30 minutes, when the meringue should be quite crisp.

Apple Meringue Slices

Sift 6ozs plain flour with a good pinch of salt. Rub in 3ozs margarine, add 1-2ozs sugar. Bind with the beaten yolks of 2 eggs, adding a very little water if necessary. Line a Swiss roll tin (about 8 x 10) with the pastry. Prick lightly and bake at no 5 for 15 minutes. Meanwhile, stew about 1lb apples with sugar, a little water and a squeeze of lemon juice until they are tender. Spread over the pastry, then cover with a meringue made from 2 egg-whites and 4ozs caster sugar. Sprinkle with a little sugar, and bake at No 2 for 25-30 minutes. Cut into squares.

Autumn Fruit Fool

- 2lbs cooking apples
- 1lb blackberries
- 4-6 ozs granulated sugar
- ¼ pint cream, whipped
- ¼ pint custard

Peel, core and slice the apples. Wash the blackberries and cook the fruits with sugar in a little water. Remove from the heat and sieve. Fold in the whipped cream and custard. Serve in individual glasses.

Baked Apricots

* 1½ lbs fresh apricots
* 4-5 tablespoons water
* 5-6ozs caster sugar

Place the washed whole apricots in a fireproof dish, cover with the sugar and add the water. Cover with a lid (or foil) and place in the centre of slow oven, gas no 2. Bake for 1 hour, when the fruit should be soft. Cool and serve with single cream, while still slightly warm. Other fruits, such as plums, gooseberries, etc may be served in this way. Add a tablespoon or so of brandy to the dish before serving.

Baked Custard

Beat 4 eggs (not too large) with 1oz caster sugar (vanilla flavoured if possible). Heat 1 pint of milk to below boiling point and pour onto the eggs. Beat well, put into a buttered dish standing in a tin of cold water to come about halfway up the side, grate nutmeg over the top (if liked) and bake at Gas No 3 for about 1 hour until set (centre shelf).

Baked Custards

(individual) (3 servings)

- ✳ 3 eggs, medium size
- ✳ Three quarter pint of milk
- ✳ 2ozs caster sugar, approx.

Set the oven to Gas Mark 3-4. Butter 3 of my brown soup bowls and stand in a baking tin. Fill the tin with cold water to come about half way up the bowls. Beat the eggs and sugar together very thoroughly. Heat the milk to below boiling point and pour over the beaten eggs. Whisk well, then pour into the prepared bowls. Grate nutmeg over the top as generously as you like and set in the middle of the oven for about half to three quarters of an hour. They should be just nicely set and firm to the touch. Serve hot or cold with cream and/or a good preserve.

*This recipe fills my 6 small ramekins (blue and yellow linings), all other instructions as above – although smaller, cooking times seemed to be the same.

Try gas at Mark 4 with Belling cooker and allow 1 hour.

Baked Fresh Pears

Take 6 dessert pears, peel and halve and remove the core with a teaspoon. Place in a baking/serving dish. Sprinkle over 3 tablespoons of soft brown sugar. Take 1oz of butter and flake it over the fruit. Cover with a greased paper or foil and bake for about 25-30 minutes, mark 4. The pears should be soft to the point of a knife. Remove the paper and immediately pour into the dish ¼ pint double cream. Serve immediately.

Bakewell Tart

- 8ozs puff pastry
- 2 eggs
- 2 egg yolks
- 4ozs butter, melted
- 4ozs sugar
- 3ozs ground almonds
- Jam
- 4 table spoons icing sugar

Roll out the pastry to line an 8-inch sandwich tin or flan dish. Chill for 30 minutes. Beat the eggs and egg yolks together, then beat in the butter, sugar and ground almonds. Spread the jam generously over the base of the pastry case. Spoon over the almond mixture. Make at mark 6 for about 30 minutes until firm. Cool. Mix the sifted icing sugar and water until smooth and pipe lines across the top of the tart.

Banana Cream Cake

Cream together 4ozs margarine, 4ozs caster sugar and 1 well-mashed banana. When soft and creamy, add 2 eggs one at a time with a spoonful of sifted flour to each. Beat well between each addition, then lightly stir in the remainder of the weighed and sifted flour (4ozs in all). Divide between 2 7 or 8 inch sandwich tins and bake at Mark 4 or 5. When cooked, sandwich the cakes with a banana cream filling: mash two bananas well with a teaspoon of caster sugar. Stir in about 2 tablespoons of single or double cream.

Banana en Croute

✳ 13oz pack puff pastry (frozen)   ✳ 6 bananas

Roll the pastry to a strip 9" x 20", trim the edges and cut into 6 long strips 1½ inches wide. Peel a banana and, starting at the bottom, wind a long strip of pastry all the way round in a spiral, each layer overlapping by about one-third of the width of the split. Each strip should be damped along the edge. Seal the ends well and brush all along with beaten egg. Repeat with the remaining bananas. Place them all on a baking sheet and bake in the centre of the oven, mark 7, for about 20 minutes. Sprinkle with caster sugar before serving.

Brown Betty

I used my smaller white fluted flan dish (with the treacle tart recipe on it). Put layers of thinly sliced buttered bread (stale if possible) into the dish with layers of prepared fruit in season. Sprinkle each layer with brown sugar, start and finish with layers of bread and butter. Bake for about 30 minutes in a moderate oven (Gas No 5), and serve with custard or cream.

Bun Loaf

- 8ozs SR flour
- 4ozs sugar
- 4ozs butter or margarine
- 1 egg
- Milk
- 1 tablespoon black treacle
- Pinch of nutmeg
- 1oz currants

Sift the flour with a pinch of salt into a bowl. Rub in the fat. Stir in the sugar, nutmeg, black treacle and currants. Add the beaten egg and mix to a fairly soft consistency, adding a little milk. Turned into a greased and lined loaf tin and bake at mark 2 for 1¾ hours. Serve sliced and buttered.

Butterfly Cakes

- ☀ 2ozs butter
- ☀ 2ozs caster sugar
- ☀ 1 egg, medium size
- ☀ 2 ozs SR flour (generous measure)
- ☀ 3-4ozs double cream
- ☀ Raspberry jam

Set the oven to Mark 5. Beat the butter and sugar to a soft white cream in a white basin, break in the egg and a spoonful of the sifted flour. Beat into the mixture, then lightly fold in the remaining flour. Divide between 12 small paper cake cases and bake on a tray or sheet of bun tins for about 20 mins until risen and golden. Allow to cool. Beat the cream with half a teaspoon of caster sugar until thick. Using a small sharp knife, cut a circle out of the top of each cake and cut into halves. Spoon teaspoon of whipped cream into the hollow of each cake then replace the two halves positioned like wings. Put a bead of jam between the wings.

Butterscotch Sauce

- 2ozs butter
- 3ozs soft brown sugar
- 2ozs granulated sugar
- 5ozs golden syrup
- 4 fluid ozs double cream
- Few drops vanilla essence

Place the butter, both the sugars and the syrup in a medium-sized thick saucepan. Heat slowly and when the ingredients have completely melted and the sugar dissolved to form a liquid, continue to heat gently for a further 5 minutes. Turn off the heat. Gradually stir in the cream, then the vanilla essence. Stir for a further 2-3 minutes until the sauce is absolutely smooth.

This sauce can be served hot (for instance with a sponge pudding) and is very good served cold with ice cream. It will keep for several weeks if stored in the fridge in a screw-top jar.

Cherry and Almond Shortbread

- 8ozs plain flour
- 5ozs butter
- 3ozs caster sugar
- 1oz ground almonds
- 2ozs glace cherries
- Icing sugar

Sift the flour into a mixing bowl. Add the butter, cut into small pieces, and rub in until the mixture is like fine breadcrumbs. Stir in the sugar, ground almonds and quartered cherries. Press well together to form a dough, turn onto a well-floured board and knead well until it is smooth and silky. Place on a greased Swiss-roll tin (about 11" x 7") and press into place, smoothing over the top. Prick well all over and bake on the centre shelf of the oven (Gas mark 4) for about 20-25 minutes, when it should be pale golden. Remove pan from the oven and mark deeply (but do not cut) into 20 sections. When cool, sift with icing sugar and remove from the tin.

Cherry and Almond Slices

- 4ozs sweetened short pastry
- 2½ ozs margarine
- 2½ ozs caster sugar
- 3ozs SR flour
- 1oz ground almonds
- 1 egg (large)
- Half teaspoon almond essence
- 3ozs glace cherries
- Flaked almonds

Roll out the pastry and line a shallow tin about 11 x 7. Beat the margarine and caster sugar to a soft cream, then beat in the egg and essence, together with a little of the sifted flour. Fold in the rest of the flour, the ground almonds and the halved cherries. Spread evenly in the pastry-lined tin, sprinkle a few flaked almonds over the top. Bake in the centre of the oven at Mark 4-5 for about 30 minutes. When cool, cut into fingers.

Chocolate Cake (1)

- ✹ 7ozs SR flour
- ✹ 2 level tablespoons cocoa
- ✹ 4ozs butter or margarine
- ✹ 4ozs sugar
- ✹ 2 eggs
- ✹ 3 tablespoons milk (approx.)

Sift the flour and the cocoa with a good pinch of salt. Rub in the butter or margarine, stir in the sugar. Add the well-beaten eggs and the milk. Stir all together to a smooth consistency. Place in a greased and lined tin and bake at mark 4 (centre shelf) for about an hour. When cold, split and fill with a chocolate filling (see either filling or icing recipes for Chocolate Log) and ice if liked.

Chocolate Cake (2)

* 4ozs SR flour
* 4ozs caster sugar
* 4ozs margarine
* 2 eggs (fairly large)
* 3ozs polka dots
* 2 dessertspoons black coffee

Melt the polka dots (or plain cooking chocolate) with the coffee in a basin over hot water until smooth and creamy. Beat together the margarine and sugar until soft and light. Separate the eggs. Add the yolks one by one to the mixture with a little of the weighed and sifted flour to each. Beat very thoroughly, then stir in the melted chocolate mixture together with the weighed and sifted flour a little at a time. Whisk the egg whites to a stiff meringue and fold into the cake mixture. Put into a greased and lined 6" square tin and bake at Mark 4 for about 60-70 minutes. This cake can be split and filled with any good filling, iced and decorated as desired, and keeps extremely well.

Chocolate Chalet Cake

* Half pound plain chocolate
* 2ozs butter
* 2 level tablespoons golden syrup
* 1 level teaspoon ground cinnamon
* 3 quarter pound plain broken biscuits
* 2 large eggs
* Quarter pint double cream
* Eighth pint single cream
* Grated or flaked chocolate

Well-grease a pound size loaf-tin. Break the chocolate into small pieces and place in a saucepan. Add the butter, syrup and cinnamon and place over a low heat. Warm gently until all the ingredients are melted together, stirring all the time, then remove from the heat. Beat in each egg separately, then stir in the biscuits ('Marie' type), roughly crumbled. Mix well together and turn into the prepared tin. Smooth the top well and leave in the refrigerator for at least two hours. Turn out using a warmed palette knife to loosen the sides. Beat the double cream well, beat in the single cream, and spread all over the cake. Sprinkle well with grated or flaked chocolate.

Chocolate Coffee Blancmange

- ✳ 1 pint milk
- ✳ 1 good dessertspoon instant coffee (powder or granules)
- ✳ 2 dessertspoons sugar
- ✳ 3 good dessertspoons cornflour

Reserving a little of the milk, pour the remainder into a saucepan. Add the sugar and the coffee, dissolve over a gentle heat. Put 1½ ozs of the chocolate into a small basin and melt over hot (not boiling) water, then stir the melted chocolate into the coffee and milk mixture. Add the cornflour to the reserved milk, stir well until smooth and add to the coffee mixture. Bring to the boil stirring all the time, cook for a few minutes until thick and smooth, then pour into a dish. Cover with a circle of foil and leave to go cold. Remove the foil carefully, melt the remaining chocolate over hot water then dribble it all over the surface of the pudding. Leave in the fridge for a few hours before serving with cream.

Chocolate Flake Cake

Make a chocolate sponge sandwich using 4ozs margarine, 4ozs caster sugar, 2 eggs, 3ozs self-raising flour and 1oz cocoa. Bake in 2 x 7-inch tins in the centre of the oven at Mark 4 for about 25 minutes. When cold, sandwich the cakes with a layer of buttercream (made by beating 1½ ozs butter with 3ozs sifted icing sugar and 1 dessertspoon warm water) and spread buttercream over the top. Break up a large dairy flake bar and scatter thickly over the top of the cake.

Chocolate Log

- 2ozs soft margarine
- 4ozs caster sugar
- 2 medium eggs
- 3½ ozs SR flour
- ½ oz cocoa
- 1 teaspoon Nescafé

FILLING:

- ¼ pint double cream (or rather less)

ICING:

- 1 teasp. cocoa
- 1 dessertsp. single cream or top milk
- ½ oz butter
- 1½ -2ozs icing sugar

Line a small Swiss roll tin with paper and heat the oven to gas no. 6. Place all the ingredients (flour and cocoa sieved together) in a basin and beat very well for about 5 mins until soft and light. Dissolve the Nescafé in a teaspoon of warm water before adding (there should be some left over). Spread in the tin and bake at Mark 6, centre shelf, for about 15 mins. Turn out carefully onto non-stick paper, trim the ends and roll up carefully with the paper inside. Wrap in a damp tea-towel and leave to cool. Whip the cream with a little caster sugar and the remaining liquid coffee. Carefully unroll the cake, spread with the cream and roll up again.

To make the icing, melt the butter with the milk and cocoa, when smooth stir in the sifted icing sugar. Spread over the roll, mark ridges with a fork, grate a little chocolate over the top, decorate with holly leaves and c. robin.

Chocolate Spiced Loaf

* 3 medium eggs
* 6ozs soft brown sugar
* 6ozs butter
* 6ozs SR flour
* 1 level teaspoon mixed spice
* 5 tablespoons milk
* 5 tablespoons lemon juice
* Few drops vanilla essence
* 3ozs plain chocolate, broken up

Grease and line a loaf tin (9" x 4" x 3"). Beat the eggs and brown sugar until pale. Melt the butter and add to the eggs and sugar. Sift the flour, spice and a pinch of salt and stir into the mixture. Heat the milk to lukewarm in the pan that was used for the butter, add to the mixture with the lemon juice, vanilla and chocolate. Mix well together, pour into the loaf tin and bake at mark 4 for about 1 hour. Brush the top of the warm loaf with melted apricot jam and cover with vermicelli. Serve either plain or buttered.

This loaf freezes very well.

Coconut Cake

- 4ozs caster sugar
- 4ozs margarine
- 2 eggs
- 5ozs SR flour
- 1oz desiccated coconut
- The rind (finely grated) of 1 orange or lemon and 2ozs quartered glace cherries
- 5ozs SR flour, 1oz cocoa, ice with choc icing when cold
- 1 teasp ginger (ground) and 1 tblsp black treacle, little bits of stem ginger if liked
- 1-2ozs chopped walnuts, 2-3ozs dates cut small, scatter halved walnuts on top before baking (any larger loaf tin for this one).
- 5ozs SR flour
- 1oz desiccated coconut

Cream the margarine and sugar in a warm basin until light and fluffy. Add the eggs, one at a time, with a spoonful of the sifted flour to each. Beat well after adding each egg, then lightly stir in the rest of the sifted flour. Lastly add the coconut. Turn into a small well-greased and lined loaf tin (my smaller tin), smooth the top, hollowing slightly and sprinkle generously with extra coconut. Bake in the centre of the oven (Mark 4) for about 45 minutes.

Coffee & Walnut Cake

- 4ozs butter or margarine
- 4ozs caster sugar
- 3 eggs
- 6ozs plain flour
- 1 level teaspoon baking powder
- 3ozs shelled walnuts
- 1 tablespoon strong coffee

Cream the fat and sugar, add the eggs one at a time alternating with the flour (sifted with a pinch of salt and the baking powder). Add the coffee and the chopped walnuts. Turn into a greased and lined 6" tin and bake at gas no.4 for about 1¼ hours. When cool decorate with coffee icing and walnuts.

Cream Caramel

- ✳ 1 pint milk
- ✳ 1oz caster sugar
- ✳ Knob of butter
- ✳ 3 eggs
- ✳ Pinch of salt
- ✳ Caramel
- ✳ 3ozs granulated sugar
- ✳ 3 tablespoons water

Put the 3ozs sugar and water into a small thick saucepan and stir until the sugar is dissolved. Boil rapidly until the mixture is a deep golden brown, but don't let it burn. Pour it into a 1½-2 pint buttered oven dish and swirl around quickly to coat the base and sides before it sets. Put the milk, sugar and butter into a saucepan and heat it just below boiling point. Beat the eggs very thoroughly in a large basin, pour on the milk, and mix well. Pour into the caramel-lined dish and stand it in a baking-tin filled with cold water to come halfway up the sides. Bake on the centre shelf of the oven at Mark 4 for 40 minutes. Leave to cool and then place in the refrigerator if liked. Serve with cream, either single or double.

To stew dried fruit, take ½lb mixed dried fruits (apple rings, apricots, peaches, pears, prunes, etc), place in a basin with the thinly pared rind of half a lemon and cover with 1 pint cold water. Leave overnight. Pit the fruits and liquid and rind in a saucepan, add 3ozs sugar, bring to the boil and simmer gently (partly covered) for ½-¾ hour. Squeeze the juice from half a lemon, make up to one eighth pint with water and add to the pan. Continue to simmer for a further half-hour. Remove the strip of lemon rind before serving. Serve cold with cream of custard.

Crème Brulée

Beat together the yolks of 6 eggs and 1½ ozs caster sugar (vanilla flavoured if possible) until a thick cream. Meanwhile, heat 1 pint of double cream almost to boiling point, then pour onto the eggs and sugar in a thin steady stream, beating all the time. Return the mixture to the saucepan (which should be a thick one) and heat over a very gentle flame, stirring all the time, until the mixture thickens, but do not allow it to come to boiling point. Great vigilance is needed at this stage, as if it becomes too hot it will curdle. When the custard thickly coats a wooden spoon, pour it into a heatproof serving dish and leave in the fridge for several hours to become cold and firm. About an hour before serving spread eighth to quarter inch layer of soft brown sugar over the custard and place under a hot grill until the sugar caramelises, but do not let it burn. This should only take a few moments.

Cut & Come Again Cake

- 8ozs SR flour
- 1 teaspoon mixed spice
- 1oz ground almonds
- 4ozs sugar
- 4ozs margarine
- 1 teaspoon almond essence

- 4ozs mixed dried fruit
- 4ozs glace cherries
- 1 egg
- 2 dessertspoons marmalade
- 3 quarters gill (1 gill = quarter pint) mixed milk and water (4 fluid ozs)

Sift the flour with a pinch of salt into a mixing bowl. Rub in the margarine. Add the sugar and ground almonds, stirring them in, then the fruit and quartered cherries. Mix well. Add the beaten egg and the liquid, stir thoroughly, then the marmalade. Mix all to a soft smooth mixture and turn into a loaf tin (my larger one) or cake tin 6" or 7". Bake for about 1-1¼ hrs at Mark 4. If liked, a few split almonds may be put on top of the cake after the first half hour of baking. (1 hour 20 mins in 6-inch round tin).

Note: Almond icing (quarter lb ground almonds, 2ozs icing sugar, 2ozs caster sugar, a little beaten egg, almond essence) rolled to the size of the cake tin used, can make a good and simple Easter Cake. Bake in a 7-inch round tin for about 2-2¼ hours, Mark 3½ for 2 hours.

Dundee Cake

- 8ozs plain flour
- 6ozs butter of margarine
- 6ozs caster sugar
- 4 eggs
- 1 level teaspoon mixed spice
- 1 level teaspoon baking powder
- 1oz raisins
- 3ozs currants
- 3ozs sultanas
- 1-2ozs candied peel
- 1oz Jordan almonds

Beat the butter & sugar until light and creamy, beat in the eggs one at a time alternating with the flour sifted with the baking powder and spice. Add the fruit and half the almonds, finely shredded. Put in a greased and lined 7-inch cake tin, hollow the centre slightly and scatter the remaining almonds on top. Bake at gas no. 4 for 2 hours.

French Apple Tart

- 2ozs sieved icing sugar
- 2ozs butter
- 1 egg
- 6ozs plain flour
- 2lbs baking apples
- 2ozs caster sugar
- 3 tablespoons apricot jam

Beat the butter and icing sugar to a soft cream, beat the egg and add this gradually to the creamed mixture. Stir in the sifted flour and form into a smooth dough. Wrap in greaseproof paper and put in the fridge for about 15–30 mins. Grease a 9" tin. Roll out the cooled pastry and line the flan tin, trimming the edges. Peel, core and slice the apples and arrange in the case, sprinkling sugar between the layers and on the top. Arrange the slices on the top layer like wheel spokes. Bake as gas no. 5 until the apples are tender (about 30 – 40 mins.), then glaze with the jam, previously warmed.

Fresh Orange Cake

- 6ozs SR flour
- 4ozs butter or margarine
- 4ozs caster sugar
- Grated rind of 1 large orange
- 2 large eggs
- 1-2 tablespoons milk

SYRUP:
- Juice of one large orange
- 4ozs icing sugar

Sift the flour with a good pinch of salt. Cream the butter, sugar and rind until soft and light. Beat the eggs into the mixture one at a time, adding a little flour with each. Lightly fold in the remaining flour and milk. Spread in an 8" square tin (not loose-bottomed) and bake at mark 4 until risen and golden. Leave the cake in the tin. Put the strained orange juice into a saucepan, add the icing sugar and heat gently until the sugar dissolves. Prick the warm cake all over with a fine skewer and spoon the hot syrup over the entire surface. It may appear too much but will soon be soaked up. Leave until cold before removing from the tin. Dust with icing sugar before serving.

Fruit Cake
(La Careyrole*)

* 8ozs butter
* 4 eggs
* 8ozs caster sugar
* 8ozs plain flour
* 4ozs ground almonds
* 1 teaspoon baking powder good pinch of salt

* Vanilla and almond essences
* 10ozs sultanas
* 8ozs glace cherries
* 2ozs blanched almonds

Wash and dry the cherries thoroughly. Sift the flower with the baking powder and salt. Cream the butter and sugar until soft and light. Beat in the eggs one at a time together with a little of the flour mixture to each. Gradually fold in the remainder of the flour mixture and the ground almonds, together with a few drops of the essences. Add the sultanas and most of the cherries. Turn into a prepared 8-inch tin. Smooth the top and scatter the blanched almonds and remaining cherries over, then sprinkle with caster sugar. Bake, centre shelf, mark 2 for 2½ hours, but test after 2 hours.

*The house near Sarlat, Dordogne, where we stayed in 1977 – I'm not sure what this cake has to do with it

Fruit Quiche

- 4ozs shortcrust pastry
- ½ oz white breadcrumbs
- 4ozs fresh or well-drained tinned fruit or frozen fruit or 2 bananas
- 2 eggs
- ¼ pint single cream
- 1oz sugar

Line a 7" sandwich tin with the pastry and sprinkle the breadcrumbs over the base (to absorb any juice). Slice the fruit if necessary and arrange in the pastry case. Beat the eggs and cream well together and pour over the fruit, then sprinkle the sugar on top. Bake at gas no.6 for 30-35 mins until the custard is firm.

Fruit Jelly

Make up a table jelly and leave to set. Chop it well with a knife, then mix in a small quantity of prepared fruits eg sliced banana, dessert pear & orange or stoned cherries, pineapple pieces, peeled and stoned peaches cut in small slices or peeled and sliced kiwi fruit, tangerines, or a mixture of soft fruits, stoned grapes, etc. Fold thoroughly but gently into the chopped jelly, then turn it into a pretty glass dish, replace in the fridge for an hour or two to firm up and serve with ice cream or cream and wafers or plain biscuits.

Ginger Buns

- 8ozs plain flour
- 3 teaspoons ground ginger
- 4ozs margarine or butter
- 4ozs soft brown sugar
- 4ozs golden syrup
- 4ozs dark treacle
- Quarter pint of milk
- 1 level teasp bicarb of soda
- 1 egg
- 24 whole almonds

Grease 24 deep bun tins and place a whole almond in the bottom of each. Sift the flour and ginger into a mixing bowl. Put the margarine, sugar, syrup and treacle into a saucepan and stir over a gentle heat until the fat is melted and the sugar dissolved. Remove from the heat and stir in the milk and bicarb of soda. Beat the egg in a small basin. Pour the egg and the melted mixture into the flour and ginger and beat thoroughly. Divide between the prepared tins and bake on the centre shelf of the oven (Gas no 4) for about 20 minutes. If necessary, the buns may be baked in two separate batches. If making half the quantity, measure eighth pint milk, remove a good dessertspoonful and use the whole egg.

Ginger Cake (1)

* 4ozs butter (or margarine)
* 4ozs caster sugar
* 2 eggs
* 6ozs SR Flour
* 2 teaspoons ground ginger
* 2 tablespoons dark treacle
* Preserved ginger

Beat the butter and sugar to a soft light cream and beat in the treacle. Sift together the flour and ground ginger and a pinch of salt. Beat in the eggs one at a time with a spoonful of flour mixture to each, then lightly fold in the remaining flour mixture. Chop a little preserved ginger into small pieces and add this and add some of the syrup from the jar alternately with the flour (if you have no flour, add milk). Put into a greased and lined loaf tin and bake at Mark 4 for about 50-60 mins. When cold, dribble a little soft icing over the top and decorate with slices of ginger.

Ginger Cake (2)

- 1 cup of sugar
- 3 cups SR flour
- 2 rounded teaspoons of ginger (grated)
- 4ozs melted butter or margarine
- 2 tablespoons syrup
- 1 teaspoon bicarbonate of soda
- 1 cup milk
- 1 egg (well beaten)

Sift the flour, sugar and ginger into a bowl. Add the butter and syrup and mix well. Dissolve the bicarbonate of soda in the milk, add to the mixture and lastly add the beaten egg. Beat all well together. Turn into a prepared tin (or 2 tins) and bake in the centre of the oven, mark 5 for about 45 minutes.

Ginger Shortbread

- 4½ ozs plain flour
- 1½ ozs SR flour
- Pinch of salt
- 1 teaspoon ground ginger
- 2ozs caster sugar
- 4ozs margarine

Sift together the flours, salt, ginger and the sugar. Put in the margarine, then work into a soft, smooth ball. Place in an 8-inch sandwich tin, neaten the edges, smooth over the top and prick the surface. Bake on the middle shelf of the oven at Mark 2 for about 1 hour. While still warm, dredge with caster sugar and divide into sections. Cool on a rack.

Gingerbread

- ✳ 8ozs plain flour
- ✳ Half level teaspoon bicarbonate of soda
- ✳ 1 level tablespoon ground ginger
- ✳ 1 level teaspoon mixed spice
- ✳ 4ozs butter
- ✳ 2ozs soft brown sugar
- ✳ 4ozs black treacle
- ✳ 4ozs clear honey
- ✳ 2 eggs
- ✳ Quarter pint natural yoghurt

Heat the oven to No 3. Grease and line a 7-inch square cake tin. Sift the flour, bicarb, soda, ginger and spice into a mixing bowl. Measure the butter, sugar, treacle and honey into a saucepan and heat gently until the butter has melted and the sugar has dissolved. Cool slightly (until the pan can be held against the hand), then mix in the lightly beaten eggs. Pour the melted mixture into the flour, add the yoghurt and beat with a wooden spoon to a smooth shining batter. Pour into the prepared tin and bake for about 1 and a quarter hours. Allow to cool for about 15 minutes, then cool on a rack.

Gingerbread Loaf

- ✹ 4ozs butter or margarine
- ✹ 4ozs soft brown sugar
- ✹ 2ozs treacle
- ✹ 2ozs golden syrup
- ✹ 1 large egg
- ✹ 6ozs plain flour
- ✹ 1 level dessertspoon ground ginger
- ✹ Half level teaspoon ground cinnamon
- ✹ Half level teaspoon bicarb of soda
- ✹ Quarter pint milk

Grease and line a 2lb loaf tin. Melt the fat, sugar and treacle together over a low heat. Sift together the flour and spices, then add the melted fat mixture. Stir till smooth, pout in the beaten egg. Stir well again. Warm the milk slightly, add the bicarb of soda and when well dissolved, pour into the cake mixture. Stir well, pour into the prepared tin and bake at Mark 2 for about 1½ hours. Serve when quite cold, sliced and buttered. This is a very good moist cake with an excellent flavour.

Gingerbread Men

* 8ozs plain flour
* 1 teaspoon ground ginger
* 4ozs margarine
* 4ozs soft brown sugar
* 1 tablespoon black treacle
* 1 tablespoon golden syrup
* 1 teaspoon orange juice

Sift the flour and ginger, rub in the margarine. Add sugar, syrup, treacle and juice and work to a smooth dough. Roll out about ¼" thick and cut into gingerbread men. Bake at gas no. 4 for 10-15 mins.

Glazed Lemon Coconut Cake

- ☀ 6ozs SR flour
- ☀ 4ozs margarine
- ☀ 4ozs caster sugar
- ☀ 2 tablespoons milk
- ☀ 2ozs cornflour
- ☀ 3ozs coconut
- ☀ 1 lemon
- ☀ 2 eggs

Cream the margarine & sugar until soft and light, beat in the eggs one at a time. Sift together the flour, coconut and cornflour. Add to the creamed mixture together with the finely grated lemon rind and milk to give a soft texture. Put in a greased & lined 6" square tin and bake at mark 4 for about 1-1¼ hrs. When cool, brush with a glaze made from the juice of the lemon, 1 tablespoon water and 1oz. castor sugar. Put all in a small pan, beat gently until the sugar is dissolved, bring to boiling point & boil briskly for a minute. When cool, brush over the top of the cake and sprinkle with coconut.

Golden Crust Bananas

- ✴ 1lb bananas
- ✴ ¼ pint cup of finely crushed cornflakes, breadcrumbs, or biscuit crumbs
- ✴ 2ozs melted butter
- ✴ 1 egg

Beat the egg with a sprinkling of salt. Peel the banana, cut in half crosswise. Coat with egg and roll in crumbs until well coated. Place on a greased baking sheet and sprinkle with the melted butter. Bake in a hot oven (450 or Gas no. 8) until crisp and golden.

Gooseberry Pudding

* 1 large can of gooseberries (1lb 4ozs.)
* 3 ozs margarine
* 3ozs caster sugar
* 2 eggs
* 4ozs SR flour

Spread the gooseberries in a fireproof oven dish and add 3 tablespoons of juice. Cream the margarine and sugar until soft and light and add the eggs one at a time with a spoonful of sifted flour to each. Fold in the rest of the flour lightly and spread the mixture over the gooseberries. Bake at mark 4 for 45-50 minutes, dredge with sifted icing sugar before serving.

Grantham Ginger Biscuits
(Aunt Alice's* Recipe)

* 4ozs SR flour
* 1 teaspoon bicarb of soda
* 1 teaspoon ground ginger
* 1 and half tablespoons golden syrup
* 3ozs caster sugar
* 3ozs margarine

Sieve together the flour, soda and ginger, stir in the sugar. Melt together the syrup and margarine, add the dry ingredients and stir well together. Form into small balls (this quantity makes about 20), place well apart on greased baking sheets and bake in the centre of the oven (Mark 5) for about 15 mins. Bake in relays, and allow the biscuits to harden for a few minutes before removing from the trays.

*Aunt Alice was Gran's aunt

Individual Fruit Charlottes

Stew about 1lb apples with sugar and a little water. When tender divide between six individual cocotte dishes. Mix together 2-3 finely crumbled sponge cakes and 1oz caster sugar. Sprinkle over the stewed fruit in the cups, put into the oven at Mark 4 and cook for about 20 minutes, when it should be crisp and golden. Serve topped with whipped cream.

This dish may be used with other fruit, such as apricots, plums, rhubarb, cherries, raspberries, strawberries, blackcurrants, etc

Lemon Cakes

* 4ozs caster sugar
* 4ozs margarine
* 6ozs SR flour
* 2 eggs
* 2 lemons

Beat the margarine and sugar until soft, pale and creamy, beat in the grated rind of the lemons. Beat in the eggs, one by one, together with the sifted flour (and a good pinch of salt). Finally stir in lightly the remainder of the flour. Divide between 2 7inch sandwich tins, well greased and lined, and bake for about 30 mins at Gas 4-5 until well risen, golden and springy. Meanwhile, mix the juice of the lemons with 4ozs sugar and stir well together. As soon as the cakes come out of the oven pour the lemon juice mixture evenly over the tops. Leaver to cool in the tins, then cut each cake into 8 wedges.

Lemon Delight
(Ruth Adams'* recipe)

- 2ozs butter
- 4ozs sugar
- 2 lemons
- 2 eggs
- 2ozs SR flour
- ½ pint milk

Cream the butter and sugar and add the egg yolks, lemon rind and juice. Gradually add the flour and the milk, then fold in the stiffly-whipped egg whites. Pour into a dish and stand in a tray of water. Cook for 30-40 mins at gas no.5.

*I presume this was the Ruth Adams who was our neighbour and a friend of Heather's

Lemon Sauce Pudding (1)

- 4ozs SR flour
- 4ozs butter
- 4ozs caster sugar
- 1 lemon
- 2 eggs

SAUCE
- 4ozs caster sugar
- 2 level tablespoons cornflour

Sift the flour with a pinch of salt. Cream the butter, sugar and the grated lemon rind until soft and light. Gradually beat in the eggs, folding in the sifted flour as you go, adding a little milk if necessary. Spoon the mixture into a buttered 2-pint pie dish, the mixture should come about halfway up.

Strain the juice from the lemon and add hot water to come up to half a pint. Mix together thoroughly the sugar and cornflour, add the mixed lemon juice and hot water. Stir well together then pour over the pudding. Bake at once in the centre of the oven (Gas no 5) for about 40 minutes. The cake will rise to the top and a delicious lemon sauce will form underneath. Sprinkle with caster sugar and serve hot.

Lemon Sauce Pudding (2)

Into a basin put 6ozs sugar, I level tablespoon plain flour, half ounce soft butter, the juice and grated rind of one lemon and 2 beaten egg yolks. Beat all well together with a wooden spoon until well blended. Gradually add half pint of milk and whisk thoroughly. Whisk the egg whites until forming peaks and fold very lightly into the mixture.

Pour carefully into an ovenproof dish standing in a tin of cold water and bake for about 35-45 minutes at Mark 4. The top should be pale golden brown and spongy with a liquid sauce underneath.

Lemon Sponge Pudding

- 6ozs SR flour
- 3ozs margarine
- 3ozs caster sugar
- 1 egg
- 4-5 tablespoons milk
- 1 lemon
- 2ozs sugar
- 1oz butter

Butter a pudding basin well. Into it put the juice of the lemon and the 2ozs sugar. Mix well together, then add the butter. Sieve the flour with a pinch of salt into the mixing bowl. Add the finely grated rind of the lemon. Put in the margarine and add the caster sugar. Add the beaten egg and the milk and stir to a soft smooth consistency. Place on top of the lemon juice-sugar-butter mixture in the basin, smooth over and cover securely. Steam in a pan of boiling water for about 2 hours. When turned out there will be a thick lemony sauce coating the pudding.

Lemon Sundae

Dissolve 2 level teaspoons gelatine in 2 tablespoons of water in a cup. Stand in a pan of hot water until completely melted. Stir from time to time. Whisk 2 egg yolks with 2 ozs caster sugar until thick. Beat 2 egg whites until stiff. Add the dissolved gelatine to the egg yolk mixture, then fold in the whites. Put into individual glasses and place in the fridge until set. Decorate with whipped cream and lemon slices (crystallised).

Light Rich Fruit Cake

- 8ozs butter
- 4 eggs
- 8ozs caster sugar
- 8ozs plain flour
- 1 teaspoon baking powder
- 4ozs ground almonds
- Vanilla essence
- Almond essence
- 1 lemon
- 8ozs sultanas
- 8ozs glace cherries
- 2ozs chopped mixed peel
- 1oz chopped walnuts
- 1oz chopped glace pineapple
- 1oz chopped crystallised ginger
- ½ oz chopped angelica
- 2ozs blanched almonds

Sift the flour and baking powder with a pinch of salt. Beat the butter and sugar and lemon rind to a soft pale cream, add the eggs one at a time with a little of the flour mixture to each. Fold in the ground almonds and the essences. Add the fruit (wash and thoroughly dry the cherries). Put into an 8-inch tin, scatter a few cherries and the almonds over the top, together with a little caster sugar. Bake, centre shelf, mark 3 for 2 ½ hours.

Lime Jelly Dessert

- ☀ 1 lime jelly
- ☀ 1 cup boiling water
- ☀ 8ozs Philadelphia soft cheese
- ☀ ¼ cup sugar
- ☀ ¼ cup orange juice
- ☀ 2 teaspoons grated lemon rind
- ☀ 1 dessertspoon lemon juice
- ☀ ½ pint whipped cream

Dissolve the jelly in the hot water. Cool slightly. Beat the cheese until smooth, gradually add the sugar and orange juice, lemon rind, lemon juice, and warm jelly, mixing well. Chill until at setting point, fold in the whipped cream. Pour into a 2-pint wetted mould (or 6 tall glasses) and leave to set.

Madeira Cake

- 5ozs butter or margarine
- 5ozs caster sugar
- 7ozs plain flour
- 3 eggs
- 1 lemon
- 1 teaspoon baking powder

Grate the lemon rind into the flour (previously sifted with the baking powder and a pinch of salt). Cream the butter and sugar until soft and light. Beat in the eggs one at a time with a little flour to each. Lightly fold in the rest of the flour. Put into a greased and lined 7-inch cake tin and bake at gas no. 4 for about 1¼ hours.

Marble Cake
(Heather's recipe)

- 6ozs caster sugar
- 8ozs butter or margarine
- 3 eggs
- 8ozs SR flour
- 1 dessertspoon cocoa

Prepare a 6-inch cake tin. Cream the fat and sugar until light and fluffy and gradually beat in the eggs. Fold in the sieved flour and add a little warm water to form a soft dropping consistency. Divide the mixture into 3 equal parts. Add the sieved cocoa to one, a little red food colouring to another and leave the third plain, adding a little vanilla essence. Drop alternate spoonfuls of each mixture into the tin. Bake in the centre of the oven, mark 4, for about 1 hour. Cool on a wire tray and dust with caster sugar.

Marmalade Pudding

- 2ozs plain flour
- 1 level teaspoon baking powder
- Pinch of salt
- 3ozs suet
- 3ozs white breadcrumbs
- 2ozs soft brown sugar
- Marmalade
- 1 egg
- Milk to mix (2-3 tablespoons)

Butter a 1½ pint pudding basin and put a generous layer of marmalade at the bottom. Sift the flour, baking powder and salt into a mixing bowl. Add the suet, breadcrumbs and sugar and mix all well together. Stir in 1 tablespoon marmalade, the beaten egg and sufficient milk to make a soft consistency. Turn the mixture into the prepared basin, cover well and steam for 2 hours. Serve with custard, or cream of marmalade sauce:

- 1 level tablespoon cornflour
- ¼ pint water
- Juice of ½ lemon
- 2 heaped tablespoons marmalade

Blend the cornflour and water in a saucepan, add the lemon juice and marmalade. Stir over a moderate heat until thickened and boiling. Simmer for 2-3 minutes.

Marshmallow Pie

* Biscuit crust:
* 2 teaspoons brown sugar
* 6ozs sweet biscuits
* 3ozs butter (melted)

FILLING:
* 4ozs marshmallows
* ¾ breakfast cup milk
* ½ cup whipped cream
* ½ teaspoon vanilla essence (or other flavouring)
* 2 egg whites, stiffly beaten

Crush the biscuits. Add the melted butter and brown sugar to the biscuit crumbs and mix well. Spread into an 8-inch pie dish, press well around and put aside until firm.

Melt the marshmallows and the milk in a saucepan. Pour into a basin and leave until partly set. Add the whipped cream and the stiffly beaten egg whites and essence. Pour into the biscuit crust, leave to set and decorate before serving.

Meringue Glacé

* 1 family brick dairy ice cream
* 6-8 meringue shells
* Quarter pint double cream
* 4 squares cooking chocolate

Cut the ice cream into large pieces and place in a cold serving dish. Break up the meringue shells into fairly large pieces and scatter over the ice cream. Pour the cream over this and then drip the melted chocolate from a spoon to form trails over the top. Serve immediately with wafers.

Milk Jelly

Dissolve a jelly in half a pint of hot water. Beat an egg. Dilute a small tin of evaporated milk with enough cold water to make a half pint and bring nearly to boiling point. Pour onto the egg and cook very gently until the mixture thickens, but do not let it boil. Leave to cool. When both this mixture and the jelly are cool mix them together and pour into a mould. Leave in a cold place to set (about 2 hours in a fridge).

Orange Boodle

- 4ozs sponge cake
- 4 oranges
- 4 lemons
- 1 tablespoon sugar
- ½ pint double cream

Grate the zest from 2 oranges and 2 lemons. Squeeze the juice from the oranges and lemons. Break the sponge cake into a glass dish and soak with a little of the juice (otherwise the cake will rise to the top). Whisk the cream until thick. Add juice, sugar and zest to the cream and mix well. Pour the cream mixture over the sponge cake. Place in the fridge at least overnight, the fool will then have slightly set. Decorate with chopped nuts crystallised fruits or orange slices etc..

Orange & Chocolate Layer Cake

(from Ann Gallimore's* tea towel)

* 8ozs butter or margarine
* 8ozs caster sugar
* 8ozs SR flour
* 4 eggs
* 1 level tablespoon cocoa blend with 1 tablespoon hot water
* Grated rind of 1 orange

Cream the butter and sugar, beat in the eggs with a little of the sifted flour to each. Fold in the rest of the flour. Remove 1/3 of this mixture and stir the blended cocoa into it. Fold the orange rind into the remaining mixture and divide between 2 7" sandwich tins. Put the chocolate mixture into a third 7" tin. Bake at gas no. 4-5 for about 30 mins. Sandwich together when cool with a suitable filling and ice if liked.

*A neighbour in Ashton Lane

Orange Crumb Pudding

- ☀ 3ozs breadcrumbs
- ☀ ½ pint milk
- ☀ 1 orange
- ☀ 2ozs caster sugar
- ☀ 2 eggs

Put the crumbs into a basin. Heat the milk and add it to the rind and juice of the orange*. Pour over the crumbs. Stir in the sugar and the egg yolks. Whisk the whites stiffly and fold into the mixture. Turn into a greased pie dish, allow to stand for 15 minutes, then bake in a moderate oven (mark 4) for about 30-40 minutes.

*This curdled – try adding the juice to the breadcrumbs before adding the milk and rind. Otherwise very good.

.

Parkin

- 2 level teaspoons bicarbonate of soda
- Quarter pint milk
- 4ozs butter
- 4ozs margarine
- 4ozs golden syrup
- 4ozs black treacle
- 3ozs granulated sugar
- 8ozs plain flour
- 8ozs medium or fine oatmeal
- 2 level teaspoons ground ginger
- A good pinch of salt

Set the oven to Mark 3. Grease and line an 8-inch square tin. Dissolve the bicarbonate of soda in the milk. Sift the flour, salt and ginger into a mixing bowl. Add the oatmeal and mix all the dry ingredients together. Into a pan put the syrup, treacle, sugar, butter and margarine and melt over a low heat until all is liquid and the sugar is dissolved, stirring to keep it smooth. Pour this into the dry ingredients, and add the milk/bicarb soda mixture. Stir thoroughly for about 5 minutes until you have a smooth and even mixture. Pour into the lined tin and bake in the centre of the oven for about 50-60 minutes. Leave in the tin until quite cold, as this cake is extremely delicate and breaks very easily. It will sink in the middle but this is quite correct.

Peaches in Brandy

Take 5 or 6 medium-sized ripe peaches, cover with boiling water, leave for a few minutes, drain and peel. Halve the peaches, carefully remove the stones. Take half a pint of water, place in a wide-based pan and add 4ozs caster sugar. Place over a gentle heat, stir till the sugar has dissolved, then bring to a simmering point. Add the peach halves, cover and allow to cook gently for 5 minutes or so. Lift the fruit out and place on a serving dish, preferably wide and shallow. Cook the syrup for a little longer to reduce it, stir in about 3 tablespoons of brandy and pour over the peaches. Serve cool or chilled.

Poached Fruit in Syrup

Choose a pan suitable for the size of the fruit you are poaching. Into it put about quarter pint of water and 2ozs of sugar. Stir over a gentle heat until dissolved, then bring to simmering point. Carefully add the fruit, suitably prepared. Cook very gently with the lid on the pan until the fruit is cooked to your taste. Gently lift the fruit and place in a serving dish. Add brandy (about 3 tablespoons) or a fruit liqueur to the syrup and pour carefully over the fruit. Serve cool, or chilled if you prefer.

Poached Apricots with Cherries

Take 1lb apricots, wash and place in an ovenproof dish. Take 4-8ozs cherries, wash and stone and add to the dish. Put about quarter pint water in a saucepan add 4ozs sugar and heat gently. Stir until the sugar has dissolved, then simmer for a few moments. Pour over the fruit. Add 2 or 3 tablespoons of brandy, cover the dish and bake in the centre of the oven at gas no 4 for about 45-60 minutes. Serve warm or chilled with custard and/or cream.

Quick Lemon Meringue Pie

Sift 4ozs SR flour and a good pinch of salt into a basin. Rub in 2ozs margarine, then add 1oz caster sugar. Add the yolk of an egg and mix all to a smooth dough. Roll out and line a pie plate (the dough is difficult to handle, but can be put onto the plate in pieces and pressed into position). Trim the edges, and crimp, then chill in the fridge for an hour or so. Spread a good lemon curd generously over the pastry, and bake in the centre of a pre-heated oven (no.6) for about 15-20 minutes. Turn the oven down to no.1 as soon as the tart is cooked. Whisk the white of egg to a meringue, add 1oz sugar and whisk again until stiff. Then lightly fold in 1oz caster sugar and spread the meringue over the lemon curd. Return to the oven (Mark 1) for about half an hour, when the meringue should be crisp and golden.

Quick Raspberry Puddings

- 1 level tablespoon SR flour
- 2 level teaspoons caster sugar
- 1 egg
- ¼ pint soured cream or fresh double cream
- ½ lb raspberries (fresh or frozen)

Break the egg into a basin. Add the sugar, flour and cream and beat well for a few minutes. Divide between four individual fire-proof dishes and add the raspberries equally to each one. Bake at gas mark 5 for 20-25 minutes, until lightly set. Other fruits, such as strawberries, may be used. Tinned fruits should be well drained.

Raspberry Cakes

- 6ozs self-raising flour
- 3ozs margarine
- 3ozs caster sugar
- 1 egg
- 3 tablespoons milk
- Raspberry jam

Sift the flour with a good pinch of salt into a basin. Rub in the margarine, then stir in the sugar. Beat the egg, add the milk and pour into the mixture. Stir until smooth, soft and creamy. Put a little of the mixture into each of 12 bun cases, add a blob of jam* then cover with more mixture. Put into the oven (third runner from the top) at Mark 5 for 20-25 minutes.

*Or put a small piece of marzipan + a few drops of almond essence in the mix. Top with flaked almonds.

Rhubarb and Orange Compôte

- 1lb rhubarb
- 4ozs caster sugar
- 1 orange

Trim and wash the rhubarb and cut into one-inch lengths. Measure a scant quarter pint water into a large saucepan, add the sugar. Stir over a low heat until the sugar has dissolved, then bring to the boil. Add the grated rind and juice of the orange and the rhubarb. Bring back to simmering point, lower the heat, cover the pan and cook very gently for about 5 minutes. Draw the pan off the heat and leave covered for about 15 minutes of so. The rhubarb should be quite soft but still in pieces. Carefully transfer the fruit to a serving dish and gently pour over the juice.

Rice Pudding
(Marjorie's recipe)

Put about one and quarter pints of milk into a saucepan, add 2ozs of pudding rice, a good pinch of salt and about 1oz of vanilla sugar. Stir over a gentle heat until dissolved, then bring to simmering point and simmer gently for about three quarters of an hour. If too thick add a little more milk or cream. Beat in an ounce or two of butter before serving.

Rich Chocolate Mousse

(two servings)

- ☀ 4ozs plain dessert chocolate
- ☀ 1 tablespoon Cointreau
- ☀ 2 medium eggs, separated
- ☀ Double cream
- ☀ Grated Chocolate

Break up the chocolate, place it with the Cointreau in a bowl over a pan of simmering water. Stir with a wooden spoon until smooth then, over the heat, beat in the egg yolks. Continue cooking for 2-3 minutes. When the mixture is cool, whisk the egg whites until stiff and lightly fold into the mixture. Divide between two dishes and place in the fridge to set. Decorate with whipped cream and grated chocolate.

Scones

- 10ozs SR flour*
- 3ozs butter
- 3ozs caster sugar
- Quarter teaspoon salt
- 2ozs sultanas
- 1 egg milk

Sieve the flour and salt into a bowl. Rub in the butter until like fine breadcrumbs, stir in the sugar and the sultanas. Add the well-beaten egg and a little milk, then gradually add more milk until the dough is really soft. Be generous with the liquid, the mixture should be quite moist. Divide into three, and pat each into a round about an inch thick. Brush over with beaten egg and make two cuts on each round to divide into 4 quarters. Bake at the top of a pre-heated oven, mark 6, for about 20-25 minutes.

*8ozs flour, 2½ oz sugar, 2½ oz butter makes 2 rings instead of 3.
Also, try 6ozs flour, 2ozs butter, 1½ oz sugar, egg, milk to make 2 rings or 6-8 small scones. A few sultanas.

Seed cake

* 4ozs margarine
* 4ozs caster sugar
* 2 eggs (fairly large)
* 6ozs SR flour
* 1-2 tablespoons milk
* 1 dessertspoon caraway seeds

Beat the margarine and sugar to a soft white cream in a warm basin. Add the eggs one at a time with a sprinkling of flour to each, beating each in thoroughly. Lightly sift in the remaining flour, adding a little milk to reach a soft dropping consistency, then add the caraway seeds. Put the mixture into a greased and lined loaf tin, hollowing the top slightly and bake in the centre of a moderate oven (Mark 4) for 50 minutes (60 minutes in a 6" round tin). The mixture could be adapted in various ways. Instead of caraway seeds, the juice and grated rind of a lemon; half pound mixed fruits; 4ozs glace cherries; 1 teaspoon ground ginger and a little chopped, preserved ginger, 1oz cocoa instead of 1oz of the flour.

Shortbread

Sift together 7½ ozs plain flour, a pinch of baking powder, a good pinch of salt and 2ozs caster sugar. Put into this 2½ ozs margarine and 2½ ozs butter and when well rubbed in knead into a smooth dough. Divide into two pieces, and roll each into a round flat cake to fit into a greased 8-inch sandwich tin. Prick all over and crimp the edges, then cut each cake into 12 wedge-shaped sections. Bake at Mark 3 (centre shelf) for about 40 minutes, then cool in the tins. As soon as the cakes are removed from the oven, re-cut the dividing lines between the wedges, so that the biscuits will separate easily. Dredge with icing sugar or caster sugar before serving.

Instead of 7½ ozs flour, 6ozs may be used and 1½ ozs ground rice, rice flour or semolina added. Or divide into 6 equal pieces and mould each in shortbread mould, well-floured between each. Bake

Sponge Cakes (Small)

Cream together 2ozs margarine and 2ozs caster sugar. Add 1 egg and beat in thoroughly. Lightly fold in 3ozs S R flour sifted with a pinch of salt. Divide the mixture between 12 paper baking cases and bake at Mark 5, one shelf above the centre, for 15-20 minutes. When cool, ice and decorate or make into butterfly cakes with whipped cream and jam.

Soufflé for Summer Days

Take 6ozs of strawberries, raspberries or blackberries. Sugar well, then add one liqueur-glass of brandy. Whisk up the whiles of 3 eggs until stiff, then fold gently into the fruit. Put into a small oven-proof soufflé dish (about 5"-6") and bake in a hot oven for 10-15 minutes. Serve with cream.

Spiced Syrup Tarts

Line 12 tartlet tins with shortcrust pastry. Mix together 2ozs fresh white breadcrumbs and half a teaspoon cinnamon. Heat three level tablespoons golden syrup in a saucepan, add 2ozs butter or margarine and heat gently until melted together. Stir in the breadcrumbs, divide between the tartlet cases and bake at Gas Mark 6 for about 20 minutes.

Sugar Crisis Fruit Cake

- 2ozs glace cherries
- 8ozs currants
- 8ozs sultanas
- 10ozs margarine or butter
- 10ozs plain flour
- 1 large tin condensed milk
- ½ pint water
- ¾ level teaspoon bicarb. of soda

Place the cherries, fruit, butter, milk and water in a saucepan. Bring to the boil and simmer for 3 minutes. Leave to cool, add the flour sifted with the bicarb. of soda and a pinch of salt. Mix well, pour into a lined and greased 8-inch tin and bake at gas no.3 for 21/2 hours.

Sunshine Flan

* 6ozs cheese pastry
* 6 inches cucumber
* 3 large skinned tomatoes
* 4 rashers streaky bacon
* 1 large egg
* 4ozs grated cheese
* 1 tablespoon browned breadcrumbs
* Quarter pint thick white sauce
* Salt and pepper

Line a flan tin with the pastry. Bake blind for 30 minutes at Mark 4. Lightly grill the bacon and chop the bacon, cucumber and tomatoes. Put in layers in the flan case. Separate the egg white from the yolk. Mix the yolk and half the cheese into the sauce. Heat but do not boil. Whisk the white until stiff and fold into the sauce. Pile onto the top of the flan, sprinkle with the breadcrumbs and the remainder of the cheese. Bake at Mark 8 for 10 minutes, when the top should be golden brown.

Swiss Roll

* 2 large eggs
* 2ozs caster sugar
* 2ozs SR Flour

Heat the oven to Gas mark 7. Put the sugar on a heatproof plate in the oven and heat for about 5 minutes. Beat the eggs in a white basin, add the heated sugar and whisk until thick and pale. Sieve the flour with a pinch of salt, add gradually to the mixture and fold in very lightly. Have ready a prepared tin (approx. 8" x 12" - my smaller tin), greased and lined with a sheet of ungreased greaseproof paper. Pour the mixture into the tin, spread evenly and bake towards the top of the oven for 8 minutes. Have ready a good ½ teacupful of warmed jam. As soon as the cake is baked turn it upside down onto a sheet of greaseproof paper sprinkled with caster sugar. Quickly spread the warm jam over the sponge, first trimming off the edges. Make a deep cut about ½ an inch from the short end, tuck in the roll along this cut and roll up firmly.

Syllabub, Whisky and Oatmeal

- 1oz medium oatmeal
- 4ozs golden syrup
- 1 teaspoon lemon juice
- ½ pint double cream
- 5 tablespoons whisky

Toast the oatmeal under the grill until brown. Mix together the golden syrup, whisky and lemon juice. Fold into the cream and most of the oatmeal (the cream should be whipped before folding into the syrup mixture). Pile into glasses and chill. Sprinkle with the remaining oatmeal. This makes about 6 servings.

Syllabub

- 1 pint double cream
- 7 fluid ozs sweet white wine
- 2 tablespoons dry sherry
- 4ozs caster sugar

Beat all the ingredients together to form a thick froth. Spoon it into large wine glasses, add a little lemon zest. Allow to stand in a cool place for at least 12 hours.

This syllabub is considered to be one of the most delicately flavoured, smooth and delicious of all the 17th century dishes.

Tipsy Cake

Take a 3-egg fatless sponge sandwich, split into three layers. Drain a small tin of fruit, place the drained fruit between one layer and confectioner's custard in the other. Re-form the cake. Place on a serving dish. Mix a little fruit juice and sherry and pour over the sponge. Leave an hour or so to soak. Whisk some double cream and a little caster sugar and fold in a stiffly beaten egg white (optional). Spread over the soaked cake, decorate with ratafia, nuts, chocolate decorations or as preferred.

Very Delicious Buns

* 6ozs self-raising flour
* Pinch of salt
* 4ozs butter
* 3ozs caster sugar
* 1 egg
* A few drops of almond essence
* Milk, flaked almonds, glace cherries

Sift the flour and salt, rub in the butter thoroughly. Stir in the sugar. Beat the egg well, add to the flour mixture together with the almond essence and sufficient milk to give a soft dropping consistency. Beat well, then divide between 12 bun cases. Sprinkle each with flaked almonds, put a piece of glacé cherry in the middle and sprinkle with a dusting of icing sugar. Bake in the centre of the oven, Gas no. 5½, for about half an hour.

This recipe is capable of endless variations. A tablespoon of cocoa substituted for one of flour and vanilla instead of almond essence makes very good chocolate buns, which can be iced with chocolate glacé icing and decorated with choc flake pieces or mints, etc.

Choc Glacé Icing: 1oz plain chocolate, small piece of butter, 1½ dessertspoonfuls warm water, few drops vanilla essence, 2ozs sifted icing sugar – melt choc with butter and water in a basin over hot water. Add essence, beat in the icing sugar, beat till smooth.

Bake plain, when cold ice with glacé icing (4ozs icing sugar), top with decorations.

Victoria Sponge

- ☀ 2 large eggs or three small ones
- ☀ The weight of the eggs in caster sugar, SR flour and butter or margarine.

Place the butter or margarine in a warm basin and beat thoroughly until soft and creamy and pale in colour. Beat in the eggs one at a time with a spoonful of flour (sifted with a pinch of salt) to each. Lightly fold in the remaining flour. Divide the mixture between 2 8-inch sandwich tins, greased and lined and bake in the centre of the oven, mark 4 for about 30 minutes.

other
Sweet Dishes
and
Accompaniments

Chocolate Fudge Icing and Filling

- ☀ 3ozs icing sugar
- ☀ 1oz cocoa powder
- ☀ 1½ ozs butter
- ☀ 2 tablespoons water
- ☀ 2ozs caster sugar

Sift the icing sugar and cocoa powder into a mixing bowl. Measure the butter, water and caster sugar into a saucepan. Stir over a low heat until the sugar has dissolved and the butter melted, then bring just to the boil. Pour at once into the centre of the sifted ingredients and mix with a wooden spoon to a smooth icing. At this stage the icing will be very soft, but let it cool until thick enough to spread. Use to sandwich a cake and to ice the top.

Citron Sauce

* 1 lemon
* 1 orange
* 2 tablespoons water
* Sugar (caster) to taste

Halve and squeeze the juice from the lemon and the orange. Dissolve the sugar (about 2-3ozs) in the water. Measure 3 tablespoons lemon juice and 3 tablespoons orange juice and add to the water. Stir well and chill before serving. This is good with chilled melon. If it seems too sweet, add a little more lemon juice.

If you have time, dissolve the sugar (2ozs should be enough) in the water over a gentle heat, then add to the fruit juices. Chill well before serving. The juice of a lime is a good addition.

Custard for Trifle

* 3 eggs
* half pint single or double cream or milk
* 1oz caster sugar
* 1 level tablespoon of cornflour

Beat the egg yolks with the cornflour and sugar and add 2 or 3 drops vanilla essence. Bring the cream or milk almost to boiling point, pour over the eggs, beating all the time. Return the mixture to the saucepan and continue to heat gently, whisking until it has thickened. If it looks curdled pour it into a bowl and whisk until smooth again – the cornflour in the mixture will stabilise it.

I made this custard using whole eggs and milk and thought it was fine.

Exotifizz

- ✳ Orange squash
- ✳ Tropical fruit drink
- ✳ Sugar
- ✳ Sherbet
- ✳ Water

Pour a small amount of orange in a glass or jug, then an equal amount of tropical fruit. Add two spoonfuls of sugar followed by two spoonfuls of sherbet. Finally, fill up the jug or glass with water. Add ice cubes if you wish.

Hot Whisky Toddy

- ✳ 1 teaspoon honey (or sugar)
- ✳ 4 measures boiling water
- ✳ Juice of half a lemon
- ✳ 1 measure malt whisky

Dissolve the honey or sugar in the boiling water. Add the lemon juice and whisky. You could also add 1 measure of green ginger wine if you like it and a clove. A pinch of cinnamon or nutmeg are other suggestions.

Strawberry Jam

- 4lbs strawberries
- 3½ lbs sugar
- Juice of 4 lemons

Wash and hull the fruit, drain and layer in a large bowl with the sugar. Leave for 24 hours. Put into a preserving pan, add the lemon juice and bring slowly to the boil stirring carefully. Boil fairly rapidly for about 30-40 minutes, but not too fiercely. Test for setting. Leave to cool for about 30 minutes before potting.

NB: The new preserving sugars (sugar with pectin) could make this process much quicker.

Syrup for Fruit Salad

- ½ pint water
- 4ozs caster sugar
- 1 lemon

Dissolve the sugar in the water over a low heat, stirring gently. Bring the liquid to simmering point and simmer gently for a few minutes. Stir in the juice of the lemon and allow to cool completely before using.

This is a good syrup, a refreshing flavour. I liked it with a winter mixture of fruits – tangerines, figs, kiwi fruit, grapes, 1 or 2 pears, pineapple and banana.